Endorsements for *Birds and Fish*

In Robert Adamson's final writings we see the man inside the poet: a man who sought to see the world through eyes beyond his own. A man who loved all living things, the sleek, the small, the shy, the wild; a man who understood Life itself.

Sonya Hartnett

Of course, you've got better things to do with your time than read Robert Adamson. It's just that should you start reading him, you'll no longer harbor any idea of what those things might be. In this collection of the great poet's prose on birds and fish, Adamson's glorious eye for detail re-animates an absolutely remarkable life in which 'nothing goes unfelt.'

Forrest Gander

Birds and Fish

Robert Adamson

Robert Adamson was an Australian poet. He was born in 1943 and lived near the Hawkesbury River for most of his life. As a juvenile delinquent growing up on the shores of Sydney Harbour, he often sought refuge on the Hawkesbury at the home of his paternal grandfather, who fished its waters for over four decades. As Adamson recounts in his autobiography *Inside Out*, his grandfather taught the future poet how to 'read' the river, advising him to 'never stay away too long' and imparting the instinctive knowledge that 'all rivers flow into this one.' Adamson never forgot this advice, even during the dark years of reform school and personal turmoil that followed, when he first came to poetry.

With a career spanning five decades and countless literary awards, Adamson is recognised as one of Australia's greatest poets. His books are published in the UK and the USA, and his poems have been translated into several languages. He published twenty-one volumes of poetry and organised and produced poetry readings at literary festivals throughout Australia and internationally. He was President of the Poetry Society of Australia, from 1974 to 1980. Adamson's autobiography, *Inside Out*, was published in 2004.

Adamson was a key player in the growth of the 'New Australian Poetry' and an editor of the Poetry Society of Australia's magazine, *New Poetry*, from 1968 to 1982. He worked as a poetry editor and consultant and established several small publishing companies, including Prism Books and Big Smoke. With his wife, the photographer Juno Gemes, he published Paper Bark Press from 1986 until 2003. This small press was one of Australia's most important publishers of poetry.

Robert Adamson died in December 2022. He worked with his friend and fellow poet Devin Johnston to prepare this book.

Devin Johnston

Devin Johnston is the author of several collections of poetry, including *Dragons* (Farrar, Straus and Giroux, 2023). An editor of Flood Editions, Johnston teaches at Saint Louis University in Missouri, where he lives.

Robert Adamson

Birds and Fish

Life on the Hawkesbury

Edited by Devin Johnston

UPSWELL

First published in Australia in 2024
by Upswell Publishing
Perth, Western Australia
upswellpublishing.com

Upswell operates in the city of Perth, on ancient country of the Whadjuk people of the Noongar nation who remain the spiritual and cultural custodians of this beautiful land. We acknowledge their continuing connection to country and express gratitude to elders past and present for their strength and creativity...Always was, always will be, Aboriginal land.

ISBN: 978-0-6455369-0-4

A catalogue record for this book is available from the National Library of Australia

Disclaimer: we have left an example of racially stereotyped language on page 8 intact. It is the language of the author's childhood and, without the author being alive to approve any changes, we leave it as written.

Cover design by Chil3, Fremantle
Typeset in Foundry Origin by Lasertype

Upswell Publishing is assisted by the State of Western Australia through its funding program for arts and culture.

Department of
**Local Government, Sport
and Cultural Industries**

GOVERNMENT OF
WESTERN AUSTRALIA

Contents

What you look hard at seems to look hard at you.
Gerard Manley Hopkins

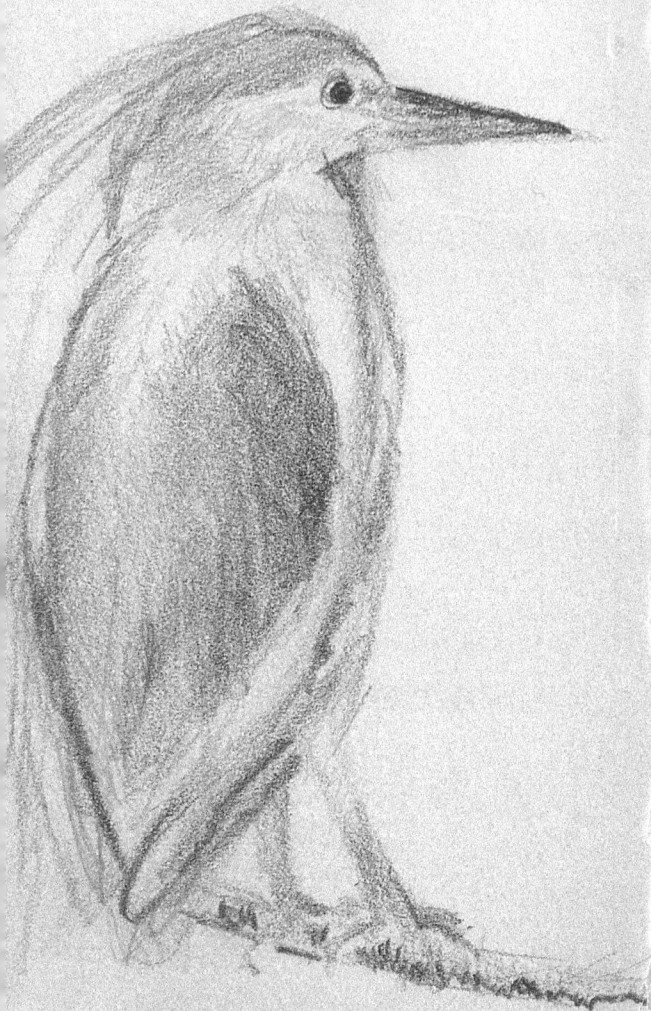

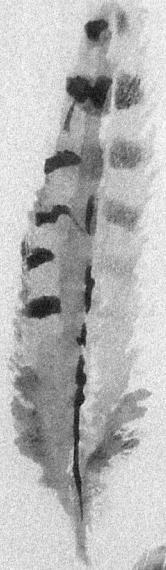

HAWK TOP HILL

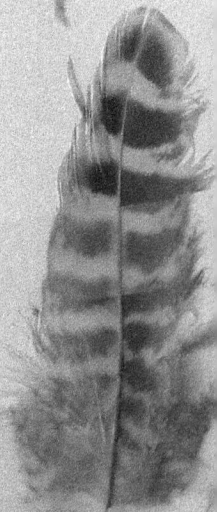

feather t

Birds and Fish

From as far back as I remember, I was fascinated by animals and felt compelled to get close to them in whatever way I could—by hunting them, studying them, keeping them in cages or imitating their behaviour. Growing up in Neutral Bay, we lived only a short tram ride away from Taronga Park Zoo, which I loved. I often went there, at first through the front gates with my parents, then later by myself, sometimes through the gates, but more often over the fence near my favourite part, the quarantine area at Athol Bay, an eerie place where they kept strange animals for months sometimes before taking them into the main zoo. I'd discovered this place because it was just opposite the last tram stop, where I'd disembark to go fishing early in the morning from a pier just around the cove.

My visits to the quarantine area were invariably nocturnal. Night after night, I'd climb out my bedroom window after my mother had seen me to bed, then catch the tram down to Athol Bay and jump the fence. I'd sit there in the darkness surrounded by weird beasts making unnerving sounds. I got to know exotic creatures: cassowaries, zebras, lions, giraffes, ostriches, emus and reptiles I'd never seen before—salamanders and a komodo dragon.

One night, when I was ten or eleven, while climbing over a barbed-wire fence, I slipped and fell into one of the enclosures and found myself, when I got up, face to face with an angry cassowary. It had a deep, resonant, furious-sounding voice: it hissed and drummed simultaneously. Booming and strutting, it headed towards me. I knew a lot about this bird from my bird book, where I had read about them disembowelling men in New Guinea when provoked, and felt disembowelled already as I stood there utterly still with the great black bird circling around me, its horn of a head fringed with iridescent blue feathers shivering in the moonlight—booming, hissing and gurgling, around and around—until finally, after what seemed like the longest hour of my life, it walked over to the other end of the cage and completely ignored me.

After school I'd often run straight down through the golf-links at Cammeray to a park where there was a sports oval. Around its edges there were lines of coral trees that would attract flocks of rainbow lorikeets. I was drawn to them: they were like flying feathery jewels—blue heads, green backs, red beaks and orange breasts. I loved them and wanted to have some. This didn't seem unusual or wrong, since they were fairly common in pet shops. But I also wanted to hunt them and catch them for myself—in fact, this was as important to me as actually having a pair in a cage. Sometimes other boys shot them with slug guns and I'd pick up the injured birds and take them home, only to find them dead the next day. I wondered if there was a way to wing them, so that they were stunned but not critically injured. I tried various models of catapult and slingshot—some made from wooden branches, others from the steel wires used in laying bricks, with strips of rubber cut from the inner tubes of bike tyres. I also tried out various projectiles, finally settling on small wads of papier-mache with a lead sinker in the middle. These successfully stunned the birds and one out of three survived.

I'd get the rainbow lorikeets home and nurse them until they came to. They'd always bite my fingers. I sustained a few serious wounds and some became badly infected, but still, it was contact, and that was what I wanted. It excited me. I wanted to will myself into the bird's head—not to tame it exactly. What I think I was hoping for when I stared into each bird's eyes was some flicker of recognition, some sign of connection between us. I wanted the bird to recognise and accept me. But as what?

I don't think I ever discovered anything in the lorikeets' eyes except perhaps fear: what passed between us was mainly a powerful red beak lashing out at my hands. When I left them alone, they'd sit there sulking, which I took to be a sign of their intelligence. Other wild birds—say honeyeaters or bowerbirds—will bash themselves against the wire, but wild parrots remain calm, if not exactly friendly, when imprisoned. In my opinion this is because, having examined all possible means of escape and discovered that all are futile, they're reluctantly but sensibly making the best of their cage.

I knew quite a lot about cages by the time I was bringing the lorikeets home. In fact, wherever I went I kept my eyes peeled for raw materials that might be used to build one. I collected packing crates and had a fondness for the giant wooden reels my father brought home. After he'd taken the lead-cased copper wire off for melting, I'd break up the reels and use the wood to build cages for my birds.

I developed a passion for homing pigeons. My first were given to me by my grandfather Fa-Fa, who lived with my grandmother Sissy in Artarmon, just near the Lane Cove River, about half an hour's bike ride from Neutral Bay. But I soon learned to catch road-peckers for myself and train them. I had other birds, too—budgerigars, turtle-doves, cockatiels, canaries, quails—and they all needed to be housed. By the age of nine I'd built a pigeon coop large enough to stand in, made from corrugated iron and some huge pine crates I'd dragged home from the light industrial sites around Neutral Bay. It had a second storey and a landing ramp.

I felt I understood my pigeons. They were free to come and go as they pleased. The roof of the coop had a hatch that was always open, and every morning and afternoon I threw some of them into the air to get the others up and flying. They loved the home I'd built for them and even seemed to know me—they came to me when I called them. I often kept squeakers (baby pigeons) I'd pinched from their nests high in the gutters of blocks of flats and two-storey houses around our neighbourhood. I'd climb up drainpipes, stuff the squeakers into my shirt and climb back down. I'd train these squeakers to home. Every afternoon after school and watering Dad's garden I'd let them out with the other birds and watch them soar up into the sky and circle around our house.

*

As soon as I was allowed to do so—possibly around the age of eight—I caught a tram and went to the Spit, where my Uncle John had once taken me fishing. A few trips taught me that my fishing skills weren't too good. At first I put it down to the tackle I owned—just a couple of handlines and some hooks and sinkers—and asked my parents for a fishing rod for Christmas. They gave me one, too. I took it down to the Spit and practised casting for hours.

There were a couple of fishing boats based near the wharf that seemed to me the most wonderful things in the world—low-slung clinker-built half-cabin twenty-footers. The men who owned and fished from these boats were my first heroes. These weren't netboats like my grandfather's, they were boats that went after kingfish—and caught them, too, with thick cord lines and red and white feather lures. They'd leave just on dawn and be back around midday with boxes of big gleaming fish—not just kingfish, but also snapper and mulloway, sleek, beautiful-looking fish with mauve-rainbow colours. I got to know these fishermen a little. They'd buy all the octopus I could catch for bait. They were the first men I'd encountered who were working at something I could imagine doing myself. They represented freedom.

I also fished around the wharves near Neutral Bay and at the end of a long jetty at Balmoral beach. I caught yellowtail, garfish and leatherjacket with the other kids. I'd sometimes get busted up by bonito that flashed in around the pylons and picked up my floating bait, but I loved fishing in clear water because you could see the fish taking the bait—you felt like part of the system.

Those were idyllic days, waking up before dawn, sneaking out and jumping onto the first tram at 4.30 am, getting down to the wharf just on light—the calm flat water, the sun, the whole world depending on the strength of a single knot. Once, at Balmoral, I caught a seagull that picked up a baited hook and flew off, causing a dreadful racket, squawking loudly while a crowd gathered to watch as I pulled it in.

I loved it there, especially in the late afternoon, when the light made everything seem more vibrant: the fig trees along the promenade, the little island with its concrete imitation Chinese bridge, the parrots that seemed like mobile parts of the coral trees they perched in, the Indian turtle-doves cooing and strutting in the gutters, the tankers moving slowly out through the heads towards the Pacific Ocean, the sun going down through gathering storm clouds, the calm before a southerly buster.

For fishing, though, I was drawn back to the Spit where the catch was a bit harder. At the Spit, there were big blue-nosed bream caught by a few older fellows who fished on the walkway of the bridge. They'd drop their baits and huge channel sinkers from a height of about twenty yards straight into a raging tide. This was difficult, specialised fishing. I tried to copy it, but ended up with my line tangled, so I just sat and watched.

One morning, one of the bream fishermen pulled me aside and spoke to me in a serious tone. He wanted to know how committed I was to catching a big bream. I don't remember what I said, but I must have been convincing because he told me that if I was prepared to follow his instructions, he would teach me how to fish. He made it very clear that this would not be fun and games and would require a lot of patience.

He was a tall, lean and nimble man, probably in his fifties. Now that I've been through mine, his lessons come back to me often. He taught me about bait and how to tie a special knot called a snood, how to make the rigs with running sinkers that suit a swift tide and how different rigs are needed as the tide slows down. He taught me to hunt the fish, to think about everything it was doing—to imitate the bait the bream were feeding on, keeping it floating above the bottom. If the

7

bait wasn't alive or the line didn't allow it to float free, the fish would notice and stay away. He taught me that collecting bait was as important as fishing itself, and took me around the bays at low tide, turning over hundreds of rocks, peering into the muddy water looking for pink nippers or green nippers—or the black crabs, or red or green—that hid in the flotsam. It took hours and involved not only catching the bait but keeping it alive.

He also taught me that there were vegetarian fish like blackfish that ate green slimy weed or leafy green cabbage weed. He would arrange to meet me at an exact time in the early morning to catch a particular tide or in the evening to catch prawns, armed with a net and pressure light. After our first couple of weeks, he allowed me to fish beside him from the walkway of the bridge. He passed on his knowledge and his love of fishing in a quiet and special way. I don't think he ever told me his name.

*

My brothers loved football and were good at it, too—John went on to become a football coach. This was only one of many differences between us. We got on well—I liked them and admired their abilities on the field and they indulged my obsession with birds, though they probably considered it peculiar—and I took Richard fishing with me and tried to teach him what I knew. But neither he nor John ever developed my passion for it.

We sometimes went to the Southern Cross, a movie theatre at Neutral Bay where there was a Saturday matinee for kids. This matinee was a big event for people our age around Neutral Bay. This was before TV. Those who chose to could come dressed up as characters from the movies, and there were prizes for best costume: free admission for four, including sample bags of sweets. I'd dress Richard up as a Red Indian in his swimming costume and moccasins and a huge headdress made from hundreds of pigeon and chook feathers (my father slaughtered chooks once a fortnight) that wound around his head and hung all the way down his back. I'd daub his face and torso with red and white war paint and add a touch of authenticity by arming him with a real bow made of privet and real arrows carved from the black bamboo I'd pinched from a mansion at the bottom of Ben Boyd Road, down near the harbour. John and I would wrap a big beach towel around him to maximise the impact when Richard unveiled himself onstage. He always got a big reaction, and since audience response was the decider, we won four times—three more than was technically allowed for a single costume.

At school, like my brothers, I hung around mostly with other boys, but on holidays I was just as happy to play with our cousins—girls, every one. Aunty Irene's daughter Pam and her sisters were fairly wild; Aunty Dorothy's daughters, Judy and Maureen, were the exact opposite: well behaved and top of the class. I got on well with all of them. John and Richard would go off to play football while I stayed at home with our cousins, drawing or playing with silkworms. I used to get them to unravel silk from the cocoons and wind it up until we had a huge ball made out of hundreds of hours of worm-work. It was rumoured that if you saved enough silk, you'd make lots of money.

Judy and Maureen, like my best friend Victor Pringle, seemed to find schoolwork easy: they came top without trying. I admired this but couldn't emulate it, except in patches here and there. I barely scraped through the recurring humiliation of exams. I was hopeless at maths; I managed (briefly) to memorise various tables but could never do any form of divison or multiplication, and remember crying over my homework, staring at what to me seemed incomprehensible glyphs. I was considered good at art, however, and often won places in school exhibitions. My drawings of birds were put up on noticeboards by teachers. I was also good at English and often came top in composition.

The year I turned ten was my best year, when I was class captain for the final term. This was the year of Mr Roberts, the teacher who introduced me to poetry and what they called nature studies.

Mr Roberts is the only teacher whose name I remember from my years at school. He was a quiet but persistent man. He liked to use memory aids such as Roy G. Biv, a name to remember the colours of the rainbow—red, orange, yellow, green, blue, indigo and violet.. This simple device appealed to me enormously, as did the notion of a name whose letters worked like a secret code. Mr Roberts would read poems to the class and go through them explaining what they meant and how poetry worked. 'The Highwayman' by Alfred Noyes was the first poem I loved. I learned it by heart and would recite it to the class.

During the time Mr Roberts was my teacher I memorised other poems, too: 'Kubla Khan' by Coleridge, 'The Raven' by Poe, and fifteen stanzas of Tennyson's 'The Revenge'. I was very good at memorising poems and was selected to represent the school reciting them on an ABC radio program that came on just before *The Argonauts* every Friday afternoon. It featured a different child each week displaying a particular talent: playing an instrument, singing a song, reciting a poem.

Mr Roberts knew a bit about birds, too, and was delighted when I undertook large-scale projects on them. One was on homing pigeons, but the one that was most admired was a study called 'The Art of Falconry'. I copied drawings of falcons from bird books, researched the art of falconry throughout history, and went into the Sydney Museum to use their stuffed falcons as models to draw from. I painted falcons, cut pictures of them from magazines and made a huge falcon collage that Mr Roberts had framed and hung up in the classroom.

Another large-scale undertaking was the project I did on numbats. I drew numbats and researched these beautiful creatures for an entire term. We had to recite our papers from memory and I can still recall the opening sentence of my numbat essay: 'Unique among animals is the harmless little numbat, whose earliest ancestors lived in the days of the mighty dinosaurs and even before the event of Man himself.'

I was impressed by this last bit, both the fact and its expression, though I remember questioning Mr Roberts about the convention of using a captial M for 'Man'. There was something about it that vaguely disturbed me. Mr Roberts was sympathetic, but assured me that by following the convention I would be less likely to distract the reader's attention from my subject—namely, the numbat.

*

When I was ten years old, Fa-Fa and Sissy moved to the Hawkesbury River. Fa-Fa, then in his early sixties, was newly retired from the Shell Company. It still surprises me to think of Fa-Fa as anything other than a fisherman, but by the time he retired from Shell he'd worked for them for roughly thirty years—first at the yards at Berrys Bay rolling out the drums (and passing the damaged ones on to Dad, who'd re-sell them for scrap), then as an all-round Mr Fixit and foreman of the yard. He also caught and sold fish on the side, and when Shell gave him a handsome payout—enough for him to buy a house on the Hawkesbury and some boats—he was able to set himself up for what proved to be nearly four decades of fishing.

Dad drove us all up in his truck to look at the house before Fa-Fa bought it. It was an old weatherboard place perched at the top of a steep rocky slope, on a long narrow double block that ran down to the water about halfway along Mooney Point. It had its own jetty and a wooden veranda that looked out over a spectacular sweep of the river. There was a huge mulberry tree laden with plump fruit, and persimmon and lemon trees; there were a couple of big sheds, three huge water tanks and a rickety ladder that gave access to the bottom part of the block, where the land simply continued until it disappeared into the river. At low tide the mudflat was exposed for a couple of hours and thousands of tiny mud crabs would emerge from the holes pocking its surface, clicking their nippers in the sun.

There was no water, electricity or sewerage, but for me this simply added to the mystery of the place. What I remember most about the first night we stayed there is Fa-Fa walking around setting up his Tilley-lamps and lighting mosquito coils. He had a continually changing arsenal of lamps he'd adapted from found objects—kero tins or ginger beer jugs or other debris he'd managed to convert into something functional. Extremely functional. Fa-Fa's lamps would work in a gale if that's what he'd designed them to do.

We went up to the Hawkesbury, supposedly to celebrate, when the lights came on several years after they moved there. It was a red-letter day: they'd held out longer than anyone else in their street against electricity, but Fa-Fa had finally given in to Sissy and paid for the pole to be sunk near the house. Even after that, Sissy never did get used to the place. 'Come to Mooney Mooney,' she'd say, 'and go loony loony.' But I loved it, even though it wasn't quite the same after the power was connected. During the years before electricity, I often stayed there for my school holidays and sometimes went up for the weekend. I'd catch the train from St Leonards, get out at Hawkesbury River station and take a bus to Mooney Point. Jenny was still a toddler and Richard and John preferred to stay at Neutral Bay where they had their football club, so I was the only one of us there.

My cousin Sandy, Aunty Kath's daughter, lived with Sissy and Fa-Fa at the time. She was going to school at Gosford. Sandy was fairly wild—it was often said that she could start an argument in an empty room—and though she made friends easily, she could dump them just as quickly if they didn't comply with whatever she wanted. But she and I became great mates. Whenever I stayed there, we'd share the big double bed she slept in on the veranda. Overhung by an enormous white mosquito net, it looked like an Arabian tent. If I was there on a weekend, we'd walk in to Brooklyn on Saturday evening after tea to watch a movie at the RSL Memorial Hall. This was one of the main attractions for young people on the river. We loved going no matter what was showing, and loved the long walk, too. There was a special magic about this place—especially in moonlight, with the river rushing out around the pylons of the rail bridge. We'd have to cross little creek bridges, where mangroves hunched in shadows full of mosquitoes and nightjars. Sometimes we'd deliberately miss the bus home so we'd have to walk back in the dark.

We'd row out onto the river in the skiff, often getting stuck on the mudflats and continuing our explorations on foot, covered from top to bottom in mud, baked by the sun, our feet cut by oysters. We liked to tease the huge mud crabs Fa-Fa kept alive in the bath until he had an even dozen he could take to The Anglers Rest.

Fa-Fa and Dad often raffled their catch in pubs. Most people did this for a cause or club, but Dad and Fa-Fa did it for themselves. Nobody seemed to mind. After they'd raffled off a box of fish at Brooklyn, they'd catch the train down to St Leonards (if it was a Friday) and sell the remaining crabs or fish in the pub next to the station.

I loved going with them when they set out the nets. When they went out together, invariably at night, they'd net off whole bays and splash the bream and mullet into the mesh—this was called splash meshing. It was poaching in the eyes of the law, but in Fa-Fa's eyes, if you lived on a river and worked it, you owned it and could do what you liked.

Fa-Fa's trawler was an old wooden boat powered by a diesel motor and held together by green paint and his will. Painted on one side was the name *Sissy* (Fa-Fa's choice) and on the other the name *Dark Star*, painted in a drunken moment by my great-uncle T.C., who didn't realise Fa-Fa had already started on the other side. Sandy and I called it *Sissy's Star*. It was a prawn trawler, but Fa-Fa used it as a fishing boat; he stored his catch on it, slept on board and used it to tow his other boats up and down the river.

He also had a skiff and an aluminium punt that served as his netboat. But it's *Sissy's Star* I remember. I'd curl up in the cabin and half-sleep, half-daydream about having a boat like this myself one day and spending my life on the river. This dream seemed distant and unreal—I knew I'd have to save for years or get a big payout like Fa-Fa to have any hope of it coming true—but the boat around me didn't. It felt like being in the chamber of a big green heart as the engine slowly pumped away and I breathed in the salty fumes of diesel oil and the pungent odour of mulloway.

It was always spectacular: the stars above and around us, set in a huge indigo dome, seemed much brighter than at Neutral Bay, and there was birdlife everywhere—wild teal fluttering along the shore with their wings just hitting the suface of the water, echoing owl and curlew sounds haunting the dark escarpments. After Fa-Fa had set the net, he'd hit the surface of the river with an oar so that it made a crisp, loud, cracking noise that spooked the fish. I used to watch in amazement as they panicked and zig-zagged through the tide, the phosphorus in the water outlining each individual in the school. You'd see them shooting out from the shoreline, dozens of them, into the net that hung like a wall of fire across the mouth of the bay. It was like having x-ray vison. Fa-Fa would sometimes let me hold the corkline so that I could feel the mullet hitting the net—and feel the thrill that went with it, too, one that I've never forgotten. Those nights were some of the most exciting of my life.

The year I turned eleven, Fa-Fa let me work with him on his trawler during my school holidays. I felt very privileged about this because everybody knew he preferred to work alone. One particular day has remained stuck in my head ever since. We left his wobbly old jetty before dawn. It had been raining heavily for days and the river had turned orange. It was a good time to fish downstream. The biggest mulloway—or jewfish, as they are also called—were in the bay between Juno Point and Eleanor Bluff, where river water hits ocean tide, snatching mullet washed down towards the ocean. The water was so dark that day they fed as if it were night. We were going to fish there, but first we had to catch live bait.

Fa-Fa knew the bait grounds at Cowan Creek and Jerusalem Bay, where the water was clear, washed by powerful tides and time spent lying in the deep valley. A fine mist hung over the surface of the river, wisps of it curled around our stern, as we headed towards them. I looked into the water, where big mushroom-shaped jellyfish floated by like parachutes in an upside-down sky. Fa-Fa called them Portuguese men-o'-war. I looked at them again: reddish galleons adrift in the tide. We chugged up Jerusalem Bay and over to the sandflats, the mist clearing as we cut the motor. Fa-Fa pulled in the net boat and

we climbed on board. Whipbirds cracked around us, their calls rico-
cheting from huge slabs of sandstone, as we rowed slowly towards the
shore, where the yellowtail would be feeding.

Then we both saw a man float up, one hand cutting the surface like a
small pink fin. All he had on was a T-shirt and a pair of shorts. Something was wrong: I noticed the unnatural stiffness of his body. This
was a dead man, the first I'd seen. Fa-Fa checked my reaction. I looked
to him for what to do next, but he was calm and told me, yes, he is
dead, an oyster farmer or fisherman. He seemed to know there had
been no foul play—he said 'drowned' in a tone of acceptance.

He pulled our skiff over to the body, then touched it. It moved slowly
like a waterlogged stump. The water was shallow and the sun was not
yet warm; there didn't seem to be any smell. I wondered how long he'd
been there. Fa-Fa held up the jutting arm and the body rolled towards
us, almost touching the bottom. Then he jumped out and carefully
turned the man a bit more, saying calmly: 'Look.'

Underneath the floating body, hundreds of prawns had gathered—all
clinging, feeding and swarming. The water was coloured by their
translucent mass, a green shadow. 'The net,' Fa-Fa said, pointing to
a prawn-landing net in the belly of the skiff next to the gaff hook. I
handed it over to him and he started scooping under the body, catching dozens of prawns with each scoop. He gestured to the fish boxes in
the stern. I pulled them apart and set one up.

Fa-Fa went about the grim job slowly, carefully, without words,
scooping and turning the handle, filling the box. The prawns jumped
around in it until their own weight sorted them out and they lay in
layers, with only the top flicking. The odd prawn jumped into the belly
of the boat or back into the water while Fa-Fa scooped and carefully
turned, scooped and turned. He treated the body with a stern respect,
similar to the respect I'd seen him show in handling a big jewfish,
holding the ninety-pound creature gently so as not to bruise the flesh,
with a care not to damage the look of the beautiful shining kill. He
handled those rare old fish like babies, packing them in ice, patting

their golden flanks, staring down at them with reverence. He moved about this corpse with the same respect, took the same fierce care.

Fa-Fa rowed back slowly as I sorted the prawns. When he reached the side of the trawler, he hauled the box up with an old winch and swung it onto the deck before we headed off towards Brooklyn. Fa-Fa went to the co-op first, to get some ice for the prawns, then walked over to the police station to tell them what we'd found.

*

After my year with Mr Roberts, things took a downward turn at school. I don't remember the name of the man who taught me in my last year of primary school, but he did make an impact. My dreams of being a professional fisherman were, I realised, just that: the money involved and the difficulties of getting a licence put them out of reach for the foreseeable future. On the other hand, learning about birds cost nothing and didn't need a permit. My mother had saved up to buy me Neville W. Cayley's *What Bird Is That?* for my eleventh birthday and, after spending many hours closely studying its pages, I'd decided that Neville Cayley was my hero; I dreamed of writing a bird book just like his. If that meant becoming an 'ornithologist'—well, that's what I'd do. But my new teacher pointed out my deficiencies in spelling and maths and told me to forget my ambition.

I couldn't. In fact, my teacher's blunt discouragement only made me more determined. Thinking that he couldn't possibly be right—what did spelling or maths have to do with birds?—I asked some of the keepers at Taronga Park Zoo for what would now be called work experience: the chance to clean out the bird cages maybe, one day a week after school. When they, too, told me that in order to do such a job, I'd need at least a leaving certificate, I was almost convinced it was a plot.

My birds were my obsession and my release. I'd wake up at about five in the morning, go down to my pigeon coop and, if I wasn't going fishing, sit staring at my birds, leaving only when I had to go to school. As soon as I could, after school or after my delivery rounds for Fegent's, I'd resume this activity. My pigeon coop was a refuge, a place where I could be in peace surrounded by burbling and cooing. I knew each bird individually, having caught and trained them myself, and was almost confiding in them as I sat there, brooding.

I felt closer to my cats and pigeons than I did to any human. I often brought home half-feral cats that seldom stayed longer than a week, though two became much-loved pets. One was a black-and-white stray I called Henry (probably after Fa-Fa) who slept in my bed and followed me around the yard. The other was a female tabby whose kittens Dad drowned one day while I was at school. I was traumatised by this, as was the tabby; I became very protective of her and tried to keep her company as much as I could during the weeks in which she cried and searched for her kittens. Dad had given me the chance to find homes for them, but no-one I'd asked had wanted them. Not that I'd asked many people: I was secretly hoping I *wouldn't* find homes, and I was furious at Dad for drowning them. It didn't seem inevitable, whereas when Henry killed a few of my birds I could accept that because it was his nature.

I was always having to keep Henry away from my birds. He stalked the finches but couldn't get at them because of their canary-wire-fronted cages. The pigeons were sitting ducks until they learned to mingle with Dad's chooks, a strategy that earned them the protection of a fierce Rhode Island Red rooster. The rooster protected its hens, not the pigeons, but the result was the same: it would rush at Henry with its hackles raised and peck him savagely on the nose.

One of my pigeons became a pet—a henbird I called Bluey because she was a blue-bar. She had a broken wing when Fa-Fa gave her to me, but I nursed her for four weeks until she came good. I fed her on mixtures of rapeseed and Farex, a baby food popular in the fifties. Bluey would sit on my shoulder as I walked around our block and would sometimes even stay there while I rode my bike, if I went slowly and kept away from traffic. I had her for maybe two or three years, until one day she was torn from the sky and killed by a sea eagle. It nearly broke my heart, but I didn't feel any hate towards the eagle. Falcons and hawks are often the 'enemy' to pigeon fanciers, but they weren't to me—though a glimmer of guilt still hovers, perhaps in memory of Bluey, whenever I see a harrier or eagle swoop down from the Hawkesbury sky to snatch up some fish or small bird. I notice the elegant circle and dive, the savage beauty of the kill.

I'd sit there in the half-light of morning or evening and dream about one day owning a falcon—training one, too. The fact that falcons and pigeons and cats were all enemies didn't worry me. That was the way things were in the natural world. It seemed pure compared to the hypocrisies of humans. Falcons killed pigeons in order to survive, cats killed both because it was in their blood. There was no third party, no good manners, no god involved—no reasoning or theology, let alone spelling and maths. Nature was blunt and honest.

Mulloway on the Dark of the Moon

I grew up fishing on the Hawkesbury River and during those early years it seeped in, beyond the reach of conscious memory. Once it's in your blood it enters your life and you are governed by the tides, the fauna and flora, the mangroves and mudflats.

Memory is an active part of fishing, not simply the recording of facts but the deeper upper reaches of the subconscious river, the places where we once had to fish to survive. Fishing sustains the soul because it was once one of the most natural things a human being could do; that is why you can enter that state of grace, that lightness of being, while fishing. It is to do with the field of being; you can project yourself back to the original lores, rites and rituals.

Forty years back, at dawn under a calm sky in an old clinker-built skiff, a thin mist floats above the surface; there's not a wind in the world. A pair of tawny swamp harriers hover and glide around their nest in a ghost gum that hangs out over the river from the ancient escarpment. Their sweet whistling song belies their predatory nature. The smell of squid floats up from the belly of the boat. Your legs are bare, your heart beats faster, nothing goes unfelt. Three lines slant out at different angles into the first of the run-out. You are twelve years old. Half a bucket of live green prawns is the most incredible thing in the world to you. Now cut forwards to New Year's Eve 1996. The celebratory dinner was a sedate but deeply satisfying affair spent with my wife and our friends, John and Mauli. On our little point in Mooney

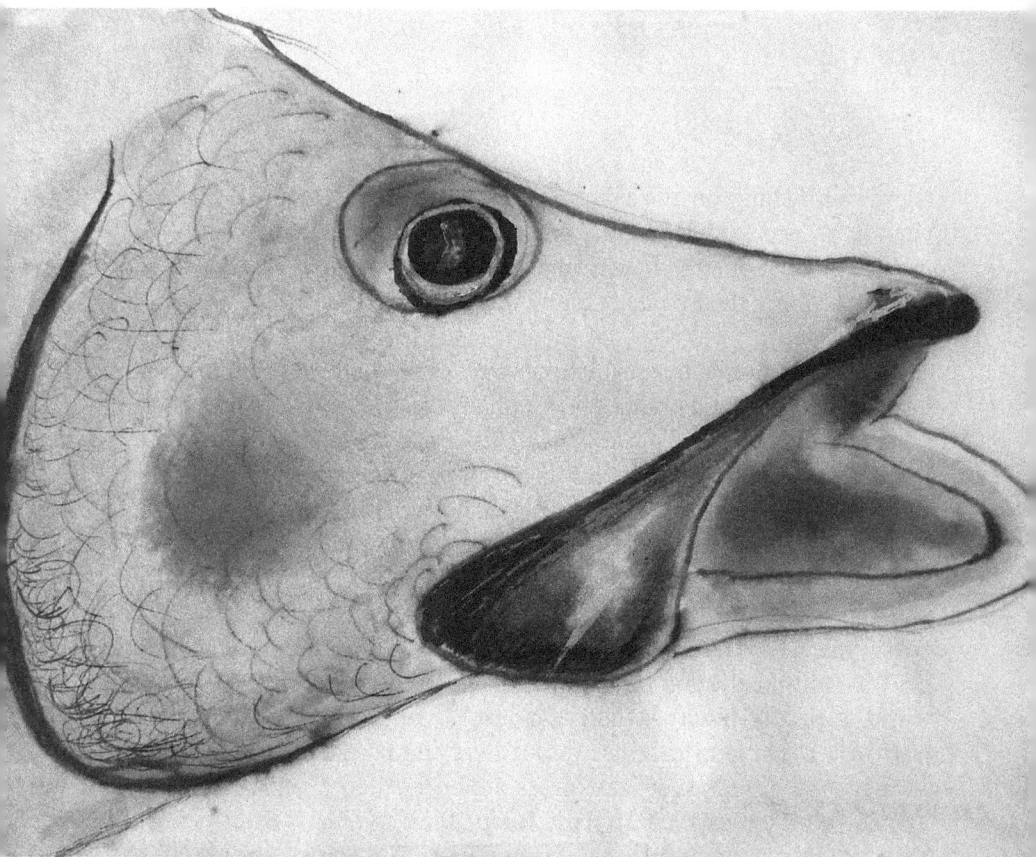

Creek, the wildest gesture to mark the New Year is a solitary car horn beeping out over the river. The kids are in bed and John is restlessly pacing the veranda and peering out onto the moonlit tide. What better way to celebrate a new year than another session on the Hawkesbury, fishing for the almost mythical king mulloway?

We set out for The Fork, one of our self-named mulloway spots, in the upper reaches of Mooney Creek. We left around 1 am with a dozen snap-frozen squid about five inches long and fifteen poddy mullet in the bait tank. We anchored up on a glassy black stretch of river on the top of the tide with a half-moon moving through the stars. In the first hour of the run-out we hooked up and pulled in just about all of the usual beasties in the river: a huge white pike eel, a couple of stingrays, a small hammerhead, a banjo ray and a few of the larger and ugliest specimens from the plague of catfish.

We fished right through the tide until dawn. We had three rods out with squid and a live mullet, but as the boat swung around before the tide started running in, the mullet kept tangling the lines. We pulled in and decided to fish one rod with a floating squid. As soon as it hit the bottom, off it went. This time it seemed to be a good fish. The first run ripped out a lot of line against the drag. We were fishing quite light, with a game line we used for its hardness, straight through to the hook with no trace. The fish stopped. Always a worry because it is classic stingray behaviour, but this one took off again and seemed to be bumping up onto the mudflat. It came in after an hour—a black-backed bullray, its wingspan at least four feet across.

We returned the next floating squid into the run-in tide. The same thing again, a great run and then nothing; it felt like I'd hooked a wall. This time I said to John, 'That's it, I'm cutting this off.' This is not something I'd usually do, but I'd had enough. The night had been so perfect, and now in the glassy dawn the last thing I wanted to see was another bloody great bullray. John grabbed the rod and said, 'I'll have some fun.' He swung the rod around and did just about everything you wouldn't do if you had a decent fish on. After a few minutes, though, the look on his face told me everything. This was a jewie (or jewfish, as mulloway are known locally).

John handed me the rod and I felt the sheer weight, heavier than any mulloway I'd ever felt—but then the giveaway, *bump, bump*. It hardly ran now. Within five minutes we saw colour, a golden shaft of sun hitting the flank of a fish. It was huge and I was so excited I struck without thinking. When the fish felt the gaff it turned and straightened out the hook. Considering the light line we were unbelievably lucky—the great fish took off again and this time as though it had just been hooked. It was still green. After fifteen minutes we got it to the side of the boat again, and this time I gaffed it in the shoulder. It exploded and we got drenched. We must have looked crazy. Talk about mulloway madness. John managed to get our big snapper landing net over its head and I grabbed the gaff and put my arm around it towards its tail. We finally had a firm grip, but the fish was so big we decided to just hold it there against the side of the boat. We waited at least ten minutes until we heaved it into the boat. It flopped onto the floor and we just sat there looking at its great golden side with its line of inlay diamonds flaring in the sun. As I pulled in the anchor, the morning breeze turned into a wind and the swamp harriers were singing their sweet, deadly song.

*

In winter on the river, July, August, when it was blowing a gale and raining, the fishermen would sit at the bar in The Anglers Rest and look out at the trees bending on the mountain behind The Gut. Old Dutch, Dutchy Kerslake's dad, Moose, Phil, Bigfoot and old Fa-Fa, my grandfather—they'd sit there drinking beers with rum chasers, and tell stories and complain about the weather. Back in those days, the money paid by the co-op for a big jewfish, a sixty to seventy pounder, could feed a family for a week. Catches of these great fish weren't rare, but they didn't happen on a regular basis. A month could pass between catches; other times there'd be four or five caught in a matter of weeks. The professionals have always caught more jewfish on lines than nets. In fact it's a very rare thing to get one in the nets: the big fish usually go straight through the fine mesh, especially in those days before nylon.

Jewfish are beautiful-looking creatures, kings of the river. After World War II the fisheries officially renamed them 'mulloway' and they are sold under that name, but most fishermen just call them 'jew' or 'jewies'. They say the first name for them was 'jewel fish' because if you split the head apart in behind the eyes there sits, like a third eye, a little pearl-like bone like a gland in front of the brain. Mulloway can grow up to seven feet and can weigh up to 150 pounds. Usually, the big ones are between sixty and eighty pounds. The bigger the fish, the bigger the 'jewel', and these are beautiful things, like a real pearl: irregular, round and sometimes tear-shaped, they shine with an opalescent glow in sunlight. The jewels aren't worth taking unless the fish is at least forty pounds.

In the winter, as it blew a gale, the old codgers remembered the great fish in their lives and discussed the ways they had been caught. All the top men carried old tobacco tins—Golden Flake, Woodbine—and these tins had beautiful designs painted on the lids. Each fisherman had his tin and some carried them around for years; some had been handed down by their fathers. Inside these tins they carried their 'jewels'. When a drunken discussion started to go on the turn, before fists were thrown, some old bloke would just reach into his coat and take out the tin. With a movement resembling some strange ritual, the arm stretched out and the gnarled, black-freckled hand placed a tin on the bar. Then the old codger would say in a loud voice as he thumped the bar: 'Right!' Things were sorted out, whose fish was bigger in the winter of '42 or whatever. Old Dutch or Fa-Fa. Out came the tobacco tins. Silence.

What a wonderful picture, these old gentlemen of the river, all opening their lids and carefully holding their 'jewels' in sometimes very trembling hands. They placed them on the bar, then the one with the largest jewel would put it back and break the silence by rattling his tin in front of the others, shaking it like a gambler shakes dice, muttering his charm or curse.

Then the barman would start pulling beers. They all had to buy the winner a middy each. Ten or so beers. Old Fa-Fa would chuckle at the thought—the night was his.

*

Fishing the Hawkesbury River is not like fishing other saltwater locations around Sydney. For one thing, a lot of fresh water runs into the Hawkesbury from the Nepean and the catchment area, and this colours the river. Some fish are more aggressive in cloudy water, especially predators like the mulloway.

My part of Hawkesbury extends from the top of Mooney Creek and Mullet Creek down to Broken Bay at the mouth of the estuary. The rail and road bridges attract jewies all year round. Some of them are travellers but others seem to live there. Two fish caught in the same spot can have different colouration—the travellers silver shot with mauve, the locals dark brown with a rich purple dappling along their back. Big mulloway are mainly caught in winter, though I caught a dark-coloured 35-kilo fish a few years back in December.

There's no mistaking jewies: the streamlined, soft-finned classic fish shape, the unique smell, the rainbow patterning on the back, the cavernous mouth with its small gibbering teeth, the silky air bladder, soft scales, big eyes and flipper-like tail. You can hold a live jewie in your hands and it will feel soft, almost warm, straight from the water. Part of you wants to release it immediately, to watch it shake its head slowly and swim back to its life in the river. Another part of you knows that the mulloway is one of the best table fish in the world if you handle it properly—that is, if you kill it with a swift blow to the head and cut its throat.

Watching a mulloway die slowly—its gills gulping for air, its colours fading—is a hard thing to take. I keep my limit of fish in a slurry of iced water in the kill tank and never take home more than we can eat.

I was about ten when I first saw a mulloway caught and brought into a boat. I was with my father on a fishing trip up Mooney Creek. We fished in the deep channel out from Seaman's Chest, a distinctively shaped rock on Cheero Point—a spot that still produces good fish. We anchored and slept there and at dawn one of the lines went off, waking me as the old wooden caster rattled around in the boat. My father had brought a mate along, and after a fairly short fight on the old gut handline, they heaved a huge seventy-pound fish into the boat (these were the days before kilos).

It was the most exciting and awe-inspiring thing I'd ever seen—that big jewie with its colours still lit up shuddered there in the belly of the old clinker-built half-cabin boat. There was no wind that morning, and the distinctive musky smell of the mulloway filled the air as I stared at this beautiful creature, watching the silver-mauve diamonds or 'portholes' along its sides gradually fading. My father cut its throat and threw a couple of wet chaff bags over the dead fish.

It was another fourteen years before I caught my own first big mulloway. I caught a lot of smaller jewies, some up to ten pounds maybe, but a 'real' jewie to me was like the one my father had caught.

One summer I was fishing for a bream under the road bridge in a rowing boat, using peeled prawns on a handline. I'd caught some nice bream and was about to stop fishing; it was the last two hours of the run-out and the tide had just about stopped. But as I started pulling the line in, I felt a fish take the bait. I could tell it was huge and was pretty sure it was a jewie because of the distinctive knocking on the line—big mulloway always shake their heads in the first run. It took the line around the boat, dangerously close to the anchor rope, so with one hand holding the handline, I pulled the anchor in with the other, a yard at a time, placing my foot on the rope each time I grabbed another length.

As soon as the anchor was off the bottom, the boat started drifting away from the road bridge, but the tide still had a bit of kick in it and I was soon drifting down towards the rail bridge. I finally got the anchor in with the boat right out in the middle of the stream. I relaxed a little. The fine line had cut into my index finger, which was bleeding, but I felt no pain as the fish pulled the rowing boat slowly downstream. In just under an hour, it was floating exhausted beside the boat. I held the line and watched it carefully, my heart beating faster than if I'd just run a two-hundred-yard sprint.

I watched the great fish slowly open and close its mouth, gradually drowning by the side of the boat. I had no gaff and even the snapper landing net was no match for its head. Then, almost instinctively, I plunged my hand down into its mouth and out the side through one of its gills, using my arm as a hook, and hauled it into the boat the same way my father had done fourteen years before. My entire body was shaking as the air filled with the pungent smell.

The tide had kicked back and was running in again. I was about half a mile from the road bridge where I'd first hooked the fish.

When I weighed it back at the boatshed it was 57 pounds. I spent the next ten years trying to repeat that fluke. During this quest, I learned to read the lower reaches of the Hawkesbury River. I discovered that to repeatedly catch good mulloway I had to try to become part of the river system itself. Among other things, this meant catching your own bait, fishing as light as possible and learning where and when the mulloway were feeding. I was drawn into the ecology of the river. I studied the birds—especially the raptors, the whistling kites, the swamp harriers and the white-shouldered sea eagles. I waded in the upper reaches of Mooney Creek scooping up prawns on the dark of the moon, pumped pink nippers on the sandy flats at Jerusalem Bay, discovered green nippers under rocks in the soft mud, and caught squid in the small deep bays around the mouth of Cowan Creek.

Thinking back on that first big jewie, one detail is important: it was caught on a peeled prawn. Another big mulloway I caught ten years ago—a fish weighing twenty kilos—was caught on a squid two inches long.

Most people say they catch jewies with big baits and live fish, but for years now I've caught my best fish on the small squid. The quality of the bait is all-important: frozen squid only work then they've been frozen within hours of capture and carefully handled; local frozen squid are better than squid imported from interstate or overseas; best of all are live squid. It makes no difference what size they are—if I set my rod at the right time and right place with a live squid, I always catch a nice fish.

Mulloway seem to be guided by smell more than by sight, especially in the murky brown water of the Hawkesbury River. It goes in the other direction, too: the distinctive odour of the mulloway is part of its mystique. I've read that they swim up under the surf along coastal beaches, expelling this odour in their excretions as they go. When the beach worms come up out of the sand to feed on this stuff, the jewies suck them in.

In the process of learning to catch mulloway, I found myself catching all the other fish in the system—bream, flathead, mullet, whiting, yellowtail, slimies and garfish. When I use live fish for bait, I choose the smaller and softer varieties. Slimies are best—preferably live, though often a fillet of just-killed slimy outfishes live squid—but small mullet are great, too. When the jewies aren't taking squid (which is rare), garfish are deadly. Another great bait is live prawns. Because they're such a universal food, there's always the surprise of the by-catch—huge bream, flathead, whiting and flounder.

I fish for jewies on the week of the full moon, especially when high or low tide coincides with dawn and dusk. Recently I thought I'd go down to Lion Island at the mouth of the river to see if any squid were around. My wife Juno came with me to take some photographs. It was a calm afternoon and the low tide was at 6.30 pm. Once we'd anchored I threw out some chook pellets soaked in tuna oil, and within an hour I had about fourteen small squid—perfect bait for mulloway. There was still about an hour left in the run-out, so I pulled up the anchor and we went straight back to the rail bridge.

By the time we'd anchored again, the tide was slowing down. There was no wind and the sun was setting. I baited up three rods with live squid and placed them in the rod holders. I usually set the rods in gear with quite a firm drag and just leave them there until something happens.

Often it's quite a long wait. But on this particular occasion, before I'd finished setting the third rod in its holder, the first was bent over, the reel screaming. I could tell as soon as I picked it up that it was a nice jewie, shaking its head and running towards the old sandstone pylon we were anchored out from. Before I had the fish halfway in, the other two rods were bucking in their holders. Juno was busy taking photos, so I ignored them and continued bringing the first fish in, landed it, then moved on to the others.

By the time the tide stopped, I had three lovely schoolies in the boat. The whole thing took about half an hour. It was one of those perfect afternoons.

*

My rod jerked wildly then bent into a steep arc. I could see the monofilament cut across black water, a catenary of green phosphorescence, trailing the fish as it plunged on into the darkness. This mulloway was going straight ahead, making a run towards the ruins of a sunken wharf. The fish had to be turned within seconds or the line would be dragged over the oyster-covered pylons that would shred the fluorocarbon leader—a situation that called for drastic action. I spun the star drag tight, locking it completely, knowing my long soft rod would absorb the shock. Then, as I pumped the line, in came the distinctive bumping of a good jewie shaking its head and, a minute later, a slackening of the line that told me I had turned the fish towards the boat.

In its first powerful run the fish had taken out around fifteen metres; now it was feeling the pressure of my rod and the locked drag. I wasn't sure how large this jewie was because I hadn't felt its full weight. I wouldn't be confident until the swivel above the leader came up. Also there's no way of telling how well hooked a fish is—and this Ned Kelly approach to playing a mulloway was a sure way to pull the hooks.

At this stage I turned on a boat-light and could see a few metres into the water. The swivel appeared and I wrapped my hand around the trace. I could now feel the full weight—this was a much larger mullo-way than I'd thought. Instead of the rod's soft give, the jewie now felt the dead weight of my hand. Straight away this brought the fish to the surface of the river and finally I could see how big it was—the whole of its body's shape was outlined by tiny sparks of phosphorescence. I pulled in another metre of trace and the jewie exploded on the surface. I put down my rod and held the trace with both hands. My clothes were drenched but the fish was still on the end of the line—it was a very green jewie.

There was nothing to do but hold the fish there by the side of the boat until it exhausted itself, and this didn't take too long at all. With the jewie alongside I could finally see the hooks: one in the corner of its mouth and the other one under the jaw. A fine mulloway—at a guess, it was over fifteen kilos. I could take my time now and watch it hovering beside the boat, its flanks dark gold, the classic jewie 'portholes' along the lateral line of its flanks lit up like crushed diamonds. In the spotlight, its head was a dappled cone of copper and mauve colour with glazed red eyes.

Juno was asleep in the cabin. However, the mulloway was in the boat, so I had to wake her up. She'd take the photographs. Already, by the distinctive musky jewie scent filling the air, she knew that I'd caught a big fish. By the time she finished the shoot it was 3 am.

We'd left home the previous afternoon, setting off at around 3 pm with the run-out tide. Straight to the bait grounds, where we caught enough livebait (slimy mackerel, yellowtail and squid) to allow us to fish right through the night. I was intending to go for kingfish in the morning but now there was no need. We would have enough fillets or cutlets from this one mulloway to feed the entire family.

The unusual thing about catching this particular jewie was that it was during the dark of the moon. Night fishing during the full moon has long been accepted as the best time for big mulloway on the Hawkes-bury, although the old jewfish lore—full moons, long nights and live mullet—has been shifting and changing for many years. Most people catch mulloway in the daylight hours in both summer and winter, with plastics and lures of all kinds, and these days some good jewies are caught on flies.

The one thing people tend to agree on, though, is the time and tide factor: it's pretty much accepted that you fish for them an hour or so either side of the tide, especially if a run-in coincides with dawn or dusk.

On the right tide, mulloway can be caught at any time of the day or night, all year round. Looking through my fishing journal, I notice catches of good schoolies, around four to eight kilos, in December each year without fail—and the bigger fish are mainly in winter. However, just to muck up any theory, the largest mulloway, a beast of a fish at forty kilos, was caught in summer. As far as moons go, I have gener-ally fished the full moon, with good catches, although there have been many cold nights and big moons without even a bite.

After catching the jewie mentioned here, I've been out three times on darks and done very well each time. When you think about it, with the dark of the moon, there are still flood-tides and their big ebbs—these tides colour the river, dragging out the murk from upstream, and mulloway love dirty water. Being predators without a lot of staying power, they ambush unwary mullet from the darkened eddies. Think of prawning, always best on the dark of the moon, when the prawns rise up from the bottom and swim through the water column—jewies love prawns.

Last month, I planned to fish the dark of the moon and try to catch a good jewie. There was a low tide around twilight and I wanted to be anchored at the jew spot before the tide started running.

We left around 4 pm and headed straight for the bait grounds at West Head. There was a light breeze and a low swell. We turned into the point near the rocks and caught a glimpse of a dark fin; for a split second I thought it might have been a bronze whaler. Then another fin appeared ahead of us—two dolphins were slicing through the swell, playing with the boat. They circled us twice and then headed out to sea.

It was unusual to see dolphins so close to shore, just a couple of boat-lengths out from the rocks, right in where we usually catch our bait. I threw out some berley and wasn't surprised to see slimy mackerel and garfish rising to the bread. Mixed in with them were some yellowtail and chopper tailor.

After an hour we had enough bait and were about to pull in the anchor when some squid turned up, attracted by the baitfish. Gould's squid are unique to Broken Bay and they are mulloway's favourite delicacy. Sometimes they are deadly when fished live; at other times, freshly cut, nothing can out-fish them. I caught a half a dozen squid using a small squid jig with tuna oil rubbed into the cloth. Sometimes without tuna oil the squid just won't attack a jig; it can make the difference between catching them or not.

We were anchored up in time for the first of the run-in. I set out two rods, one with a live slimy, the other with a squid. Usually I leave my rods in the holders because mulloway don't muck about, they hit the bait, knock it a couple of times and run hard, hooking themselves. This way you avoid catching the smaller soapies—undersized jewies that grab at the baits. These juvenile fish usually take the squid but don't bother with live baits like slimy mackerel. Large bream sometimes attack a live bait, and you can often catch them on bottle or cut squid. There arc lots uf hammerhead and Port Jackson sharks in the river.

The Dark ribbon-fish

Pike Eels grow to over two meters and
weigh up to fifteen kilo

We often hook hammers, and you can always tell them because as soon as they are hooked they rise to the surface and fight it out there.

After about ten minutes, both rods bent over and I had a double hook-up, this time pike eels. These creatures will swallow jewie baits, then take off after they have hooked themselves; their run is very similar to a mulloway, even down to bumping the line with much head shaking.

One of the traditional drawbacks of fishing the Hawkesbury at night has been plagues of catfish. Mysteriously, they have gradually vanished from the river's mouth and lower reaches over the past decade. Sounds like good news, but the disappearance of so many fish, no matter what species, is not a sign of a healthy system. As if to underline this point, the catties have been replaced by another pest, arriving in plague proportions: huge pike eels. These are usually over a metre long and can weigh up to around ten kilos. They have long triangular teeth in the roof of their mouths, along the volmer, a bone connected to their nasal canals, giving them an ability to home in on their food quickly. Their elongated bodies are similar to hairtail—however, unlike hairtail (feeble out of the water), pike eels move swiftly and are extremely strong. If they don't bite through your trace, don't bring them into the boat or they will bite you. I've heard people swear they go for human arms and legs as deliberately as a snake. And never bring them into a boat at night; my advice is to cut them off before they break the surface.

By the time I got rid of the pike eels and re-baited, I decided to save the squid and use fillets of slimy; the squid would be handy if the jewies came on. I don't like keeping the squid on ice, and so if the weather's not too hot, I wrap them in wet cotton cloth. This way they don't lose their oils and the ink that turns on the jewies. Also, baits should never be left soaking on the end of lines for longer than around fifteen minutes, as the salt water bleaches out all the fish-attracting odour.

I check the baits every ten minutes and make sure they are still sitting on the hooks correctly. Mulloway are stimulated by a moving bait, and often you get a run as soon as the sinker hits the bottom. There wasn't another boat in sight when we arrived; an hour later there were three boats anchored in a line out from the point. These thrillseekers insist on getting as close to each other as possible, so that if someone did hook up with a decent fish, there would be anchor ropes involved in landing their catch.

The tide had been running up for two hours and there'd been no bites, not even from eels, sharks or stingrays; things were very quiet. Juno was in the cabin reading a book, enjoying the gently lapping tide, the stars white points in the dark sky, and a pair of nightjars were making eerie chuckling calls along the escarpments. I was thinking maybe we should call it a night and pull up the anchor. Then I heard some excitement coming from the boat closest to us: they were onto a fish. Another pike eel probably, I thought to myself, but then saw someone making a gaff shot. The next thing, a large fish that looked like a silver log was being lifted over the side of their boat. Illuminated by a yellow torch beam, I saw a man holding a very large mulloway in his arms while his crew cheered him on.

I'd been caught unawares: for the previous half hour the lines had gone unattended. I hadn't bothered to change the baits and I'd almost given up on catching a jewie. In mulloway fishing, morale is all—well, as important as position and bait. And if you decide the fish aren't there, you may as well forget catching one. What I mean by morale is you must believe you are going to catch a mulloway. Somehow you must stay alert; if there is a knack to catching a good jewfish, it comes in the quality of attention you are able to muster. Attention to everything. I must say, though, there's nothing more likely to get my attention than to see a man in the boat next to mine pull a large mulloway over its side.

The jewies were on. If the breamers in the boat next door could catch one, then so could I. My instinct took over and I started acting on experience. Everything I knew was telling me to go lighter, so I pulled in all the lines. Now I decided to use one rod—my oldest, that I'd made up for jewies twenty years ago—and squid for bait. I looked into the bait tank: there was only one squid still alive, another sign that I'd not had my eye on the ball. It was about eight inches long, just right for my hooks. I also dropped down to a lighter sinker, just heavy enough to take the squid down to the bottom gradually.

The squid sunk slowly through thirty feet of water. This was a shallow channel by the side of a reef where the fish came to feed at night. There was an eddy swirling around from the water hitting the point. The tide wasn't moving fast and it looked fishy, like a lazy whirlpool. I felt the sinker bounce on the soft mud and then let out a little more line. Within a few minutes a solid fish picked up the squid, shook its head and then hammered it. It took out a few metres, and as soon as I could feel the weight I pulled back hard; the rod jerked in my hands, and I was connected to another mulloway on the dark of the moon.

After the Deluge

After torrential rain the mountains glisten. On the sandstone escarpments orange flakes of iron ore rust in the sun. The river turns a dirty milk from the run-off. When the tide comes up from Broken Bay, a translucent layer of salt water floats on the top of the fresh from the rain. Powerful eddies form and draw shoals of mullet into spiralling pockets of tide. Mulloway, wolves of the river, circle these trapped schools of fish, picking off the stragglers with precision teamwork. After dusk in the still air, a full moon reflects across the river as it moves between the mountains—a stream of mercury. Above the swirling mullet, a pair of white-shouldered sea eagles swing into avoidance manoeuvres and bark at the friarbirds who mob them. Today around dusk I watched as a letter-winged kite hovered above the tide: stationed neatly in the air, it held this position for five minutes before deciding not to swoop.

traditional fishing nets

Nets and Traps

I'm not sure whether David Rankin or his paintings—at the time, abstract and calligraphic landscapes—first moved into our flat, but both were part of the household after a few weeks. It was 1967, and I was living in Lilli Pilli, in southern Sydney, with my girlfriend Denise. David was teaching part time, but not enjoying it, and I was in need of income, so we started discussing ways to earn a living that left time and energy for poetry and painting. We began to have long conversations about fishing. The more we talked, the more I convinced us both that if we could get a boat, my grandfather Fa-Fa would see that we were serious and give us a couple of nets to get us started. We'd be able to apply for a fishing licence and work out of Port Hacking.

I told David some stories about how Dad and Fa-Fa raffled their fish by the box in pubs, about Fa-Fa making his own nets and tanning them with wattle bark, about our bathtub full of huge mudcrabs, and about Dad skinning eels with his teeth instead of a pair of pliers. David remembered stories from his father, about skinning fish and preparing jugged eels back in Plymouth, England; he understood poems like Ted Hughes's 'The Pike'. David had a practical side (he was a handy carpenter) but he also had the gift of the gab and would be able to talk around the authorities. With the combination of my fishing knowledge and his front, we'd be able to convince the fisheries inspector to give us a fishing licence, no problem.

But before we could apply we had to have a boat and nets. Licences were allocated to the vessel and its equipment as well as to the fishermen who worked it. So one day, I left David looking for a second-hand boat in the *Trading Post* while I drove up the river to tell Fa-Fa about our plan. He just smiled and shook his head slightly, though he did give me one spare mesh-net, advising me to start out small, supplying fish for our own household and our friends.

When I got back with the net, it was dark outside and there was a storm, or at least heavy rain, brewing. David and Den were finishing dinner. I spilled the net from its chaff bag and spread it across the floor. The weather, I told David, was perfect. No-one would be crazy enough to go poaching in Little Turriell Bay on a night like this—all the more reason we should do it. This storm would be our cover. It must have been years since anyone had dared poach this bay—it was too built up, any poachers would be spotted—but there'd be big, beautiful bream down there, and whiting feeding on the flats; there'd be hundreds of mullet schooling. And the residents would be indoors.

We worked out a plan: we'd pack the net into an old suitcase so that it would float, then David—because he was taller and could swim—would wade out into the bay, guiding the suitcase and feeding out the net. I'd be the anchorman, standing onshore holding the corkline in my hand and with the leadline under my foot; we'd string the net across one corner of the bay at high tide, then wait until the tide was halfway out before walking towards it, frightening fish into the mesh. We'd be selective and target quality fish—the bream, flounder and whiting feeding on the flats at high tide. I didn't want to think about sharks and left them unmentioned.

High tide was at 2 am. By that time the elements were working in our favour: it was almost pitch black outside; there was a strong wind blowing and rain was pelting down. We clambered down the track to the bay at about 2.30 am and, in the dark, worked out where to shoot the net. Then David waded in.

Our plan worked perfectly—David towing the suitcase beside him and feeding out the net—for about fifteen metres. Then the suitcase began sinking. David heroically dredged it up and put it on his head before wading into deeper water. Up to his chest in it, with the suitcase on his head and the net trailing behind him, he looked like some sort of tribesman.

Without warning, fish started hitting the mesh. We both felt them: the sensation of fish struggling, thrashing about in a net, must touch some primitive instinct. When it happens, your body rushes with adrenaline and your heart beats faster. Then suddenly the net went very tight. I could feel a huge weight struggling. The thought that it might be a shark frightened the shit out of me. Then I heard David's curses over the wind and rain, and the sound of spluttering. I found out later he'd hurt his ankle; the net was tangled around his shoulder and he couldn't get it loose. But all I knew at the time was that the wind and rain were worsening, the ropes were cutting into my hands and the weight of the net was starting to drag me into the bay. I let go.

I heard more spluttering and cursing as the net went slack: David had struggled free of the net but had swallowed a lot of water. I ran across the sand flat to find him sitting on the shoreline with his head between his knees. I thumped him on the back, and once he recovered we pulled in the net. There were still a few stray mullet and bream tangled in it, struggling, as we fed it back into the salvaged suitcase.

'What on earth has happened?' Denise asked as we trudged through the door, waterlogged and bedraggled. 'Are you two maniacs all right?'

David plonked the net down on the kitchen floor. 'There you go, Den,' he said. 'We've caught a decent feed.'

*

David soon found a boat in the *Trading Post* that was within his price range. It was moored in the Georges River, near Tom Uglys Bridge.

It was a sixteen-foot clinker-built launch with a little Chapman Pup one-cylinder motor. It looked great—the planks were tight and there was no water in the bilge—but it took ten minutes to start the motor by spinning the flywheel with a greasy belt, and when it finally did fire and started chugging, it gave off an enormous cloud of smoke. The owner reassured us the motor was only smoking because it hadn't been started for a few months. This was plausible, so we took the boat for a spin.

It took fifteen minutes for the motor to stop smoking, but it did stop, and seemed to get better the longer it ran. I thought the smoking was due to too much oil in the fuel mix. When David asked my opinion, I told him that as far as I could tell, it was a great buy.

We chugged around for an hour or so, checked that the hull hadn't taken any water, then went back to the boatshed. David paid for it on the spot. The bloke offered to rent us a trailer to get it back to Lilli Pilli. We drove back home with big smiles on our faces, bursting to tell Denise the news. When we told her that we'd decided to save money on the trailer by sailing the boat back, she told us that this was a totally hairbrained idea. She'd give us the money for the trailer, she said. She had a point: the journey involved motoring out through the mouth of the Georges River, across Botany Bay, and into the Port Hacking River.

But why spend money when you didn't have to? And why forgo the chance of a good long first ride in our boat as its new owners, with fishing along the way? If we left Tom Uglys at 6 am, we'd get to Lilli Pilli before dark no matter what happened. We could leave the car at the boatshed then get a friend to drive us back to collect it. Nothing could possibly go wrong, so long as we had enough petrol to get from Tom Uglys back around the coast to Port Hacking. We decided it would take about six hours.

I like to think we looked at maps, but I have no idea what our calculations were based on. We stocked up on water and supplies and I bought a fishing rod to troll for striped tuna and kingfish as we motored through the heads. We decided we'd leave on Tuesday morning, assuring Denise we'd be home for dinner that evening, and set off before dawn. We didn't tell the bloke we bought the boat from what we were doing, thus ignoring the first rule of taking a boat out into open sea. Another rule we ignored was to do with life jackets. We had none.

We had trouble trying to start the motor. Both of us were worn out before we left the pontoon. After ten minutes of flooding the motor, we got the familiar cloud of smoke, and then, after another fifteen minutes of spinning the flywheel with the petrol turned off, the motor fired into life and we put-putted away.

It was a beautiful windless morning. The tide was coming in as we cruised down the Georges River and across Botany Bay; the ocean, as we passed Inscription Point, was calm with a glassy swell. We could see the oil refinery at Kurnell smoking in the distance. I threw a feathered lure into our little wake and set the rod into position as we chugged towards open sea. I felt wonderful: going out into the ocean always gives me a feeling of liberation. David was smiling, too, and the little motor was sounding better the further out we went.

But it wasn't smelling too good: it smelled as if it was overheating. I checked the water-cooling outlet and discovered that it was producing a jet of steam rather than a stream of warm water, so we pulled the cover off to take a look. It seemed to be getting hotter as we watched, as if it might blow up at any moment. We'd been going for about two hours by now, with another four to go.

We decided to turn it off. I cut the spark to the cylinder, but the motor kept going—it was so hot the petrol was exploding in the head without the need for a spark—so I pulled the lead of the spark plug. Still the little Chapman kept on firing, so I cut the petrol. Finally it shuddered to a stop.

I suggested there might be a blockage in the cooling system but didn't have a clue what to do about it: we poked a length of wire into the water-cooling outlet, hoping that might change something, and waited until the motor cooled down before starting it again.

We were well out to sea by now. The tide was taking the boat along the coast—but north, rather than south to Port Hacking, and also, steadily, back to shore. La Perouse had slipped around the corner and a prospect of Little Bay and Long Bay had opened up. There was a sea breeze blowing. We waited in silence for the motor to cool, then tried to start it again, taking it in turns to wrap the oily belt around the flywheel and pull, over and over. But there was no sign of life from it, not even a smoky cough. It was dead.

We kept trying until aching shoulders and nausea from the sun forced us to admit defeat. Because it was a weekday, there were no weekend fishermen around, no runabouts or sailing boats. 'Okay,' said David, 'we'll have to start rowing.' We slid the oars into the rowlocks and put our backs into it, rowing for half an hour or so. We didn't seem to be getting anywhere, but it took the edge off our panic. Then one of the oars snapped—it was full of dry rot. Things weren't looking too good.

We were drifting towards the headland now, between Little Bay and Henry Head, where the land met the ocean in a steep rocky cliff, at the base of which huge waves were breaking. The breeze had stiffened and conspired with the tide to draw us steadily towards it.

We knew we were in danger, that our boat was likely to be smashed to bits, with us on board, and I knew that in such a situation, panic could be deadly. Even so, we were much calmer that I thought we should be: we began talking about poets and painters. This seemed to be such a strange thing to be doing, I even commented on it. 'Well,' David said, 'if Ian Fairweather was here, he'd be doing the same thing. If you can't actually paint, the next best thing is to be talking about it.'

I remembered some reproductions David had shown me of Fair-weather's work the week before. David considered him one of Australia's greatest painters, but he hadn't mentioned Fairweather only because he admired his art. Fairweather, he explained, had been shipwrecked and survived—and his work had grown richer, more intense, as a result.

We discussed the possibility of drowning, but we both felt we had too much left to do. This conversation felt even more disconnected from our situation, more unreal, than our talk about poetry and painting.

But by now, reality and our connection with it was only twenty metres off and getting closer: the boat was certainly going to be thrown against the rocks. 'Get ready,' David said as the boat began to see-saw, 'and as soon as we come close enough, we'll pick a rock and jump.'

We were both at the front of the boat waiting for the right moment when I remembered my fishing rods and went back to collect them. Just as I'd grabbed them and was on my way back to the bow, the boat became airborne. I slipped forwards and the rods shot off, like spears, into the suds thumping and hissing against the rocks. 'Let's go!' yelled David. 'I'll jump first.'

The boat was lurching, almost cartwheeling it felt like, towards some jagged black rocks as he jumped—and landed, too, on a huge boulder covered in barnacles and kelp. The boat moved back with the pull of the tide, then surged forwards again. I was at the prow, ready to jump, but the boat crashed straight down onto the rock David was clinging to—right across his back—then another wave hurled the boat forwards, tipping me over the side.

The next thing I saw was David, one hand extended towards me, the other clutching a huge arm of kelp embedded in the rock. On the other side of this boulder, our boat was being smashed to pieces. David grabbed my arm and helped me up, and we dragged ourselves, coughing and spluttering, away from the breakers, oblivious to the ribbon cuts from the barnacles and mussels.

It took at least fifteen minutes for us to catch our breath. We crawled around the ledge until we found a platform and a trail leading up the side of the cliff—probably made by rock-hopping fishermen. We followed it slowly up the steep cliff.

At the top we emerged onto a golf course. It seemed a ridiculous thing to find, but not unwelcome. As we walked up to the front door of the clubhouse, soaking wet and with bad lacerations on our legs and arms, a couple of blokes loomed up and wanted to know who we were: we might have been escaped loonies or crims (Long Bay was nearby). David took control straight away and explained that we'd had a shipwreck. They led us inside, rugged us up and let us dry out in front of the fire they had going in the clubhouse.

After a while David rang for a cab. It was a fair hike to Lilli Pilli and the cab fare was far more than we could afford—Denise helped us out. David later joked that the ride home had cost more than the boat.

*

Late in 1969, I got to know Tony Coleing, a Balmain sculptor who lived nearby. I began visiting him to watch him work. I was intrigued by his large welded metal constructions and whimsical conceptual artefacts: some, inflated with gas, were like indoor clouds.

Tony knew a lot about fishing. He'd lived in Europe in the mid-1960s and had worked as a cod fisherman in the North Sea, one of the hardest places in the world to learn how to fish. He knew the right questions to ask and didn't believe me for a moment when I told him that David Rankin and I had done very well a few years back poaching in Port Hacking River. I told him I was thinking of taking up fishing again and described the huge fish traps my mate used up the Hawkesbury. He didn't seem to believe that either, so I drew some diagrams and explained that they could be used to catch bream. I'd told the truth this time—I'd actually worked with a friend of Fa-Fa's, who used these traps—and because bream were worth a few quid, Tony began to take an interest.

I drove him down to Middle Harbour at dawn one morning and showed him my spots: the Spit, right around past Powder Hulk Bay, and into the inner harbour as far as Primrose and Tunks parks. It looked very tempting—enough to tip the balance with Tony—so we went back and started constructing a couple of huge fish traps about four or five feet across. Tony had all the metal rods and galvanised wire we needed and after a few days of welding, cutting and snipping we had two solid, functional and serious-looking fish traps, with special bait cages inside them. One door provided access to the bait cage so you could slide in the bait, another gave you access to the catch.

The fishermen on the Hawkesbury caught stripy tuna to use as bait, but we had no way of doing that, nor could we afford to buy any. I suggested paying a visit to the local butchers to get their offal—guts, bones, buckets of blood, bullocks' hearts, tails—stuff they'd be happy to give away. It all looked hideous and had a smell to match. We loaded it into the back of Tony's ute under some tarpaulins, along with the two fish traps and a small rowing punt we borrowed from a friend of Tony's. We set off from Castlecrag the next morning around 4 am.

We unpacked our gear—long lengths of rope to lower and raise the traps, grappling hooks, fish boxes, fishing knives—and the bait, then slid the punt out into the bay. It was about eight feet long and sat very low in the water; once we'd loaded it up and had climbed aboard ourselves, it sat even lower. But it was a calm morning. There was a mist hanging just above the still, reflective surface of the harbour as we rowed out towards Powder Hulk Bay.

I'd already chosen the spot to set the first trap. It took us about half an hour to get there, stroking the oars gently so as not to rock the boat. We squeezed the bait into place and lowered the trap. A faint wake of bullocks' blood traced its descent.

'Great berley,' one of us commented. 'Good stuff—that'll bring 'em on.'

We rowed back in the cold mist and sat on the bank until we decided enough time had passed—that the bream would be swarming in there by now, driven into a feeding frenzy by the blood. We headed out to where we'd set the trap and pulled it up slowly, inch by inch, the rope cutting into our hands, until we finally had it in the boat. We were both expecting to see our first catch, but there was nothing—not even a leatherjacket or catfish. Maybe they were travellers. Silence.

There was nothing we could do but row back across the harbour towards Castlecrag, black blood dripping in our wake from the fish trap. We began to row even more carefully; we'd taken in a fair bit of water and the boat was barely clearing the surface. But the mist was lifting and the sun was coming up, so we also had to hurry—I was worried about fishing inspectors. Out in the middle of the indigo bay, the trail of blood we were generating looked decidedly creepy.

We both saw it at the same time: the big white triangle of a shark's dorsal—and then another one behind it, two fins—breaking the dark glass about twenty yards away and approaching. We looked at one another in silence. Then I mumbled something. 'What … ?'

'Nothing, that's what,' Tony responded. 'Don't move that fucking oar. Don't even move your little finger.'

The fins, though they were yards apart, belonged to a single shark. It cruised right up alongside our boat, with its small, small freeplay—a monster bronze whaler patrolling this perfect setting, this deep blue water it owned. It turned slightly, showing gills covered in sea-lice— white doctors. One gill trailed a long piece of thick fishing line and twitched slightly. Then it turned an eye on us.

'We're dead if we move so much as a quarter of an inch,' whispered Tony.

I knew this already. I tried to stop my feet shaking by pressing them together, but couldn't help noticing the bullock heart squeezed against the side of the cage nearest the water. Globules of dark blood were dripping from it, plop-plopping into the bay. Tony and I were scarcely breathing. The shark kept moving at a steady pace, until finally it flicked its tail and lazily descended.

We waited five minutes or so, then started rowing as hard as we could. We went around in circles for a while, then gradually calmed down and began to co-ordinate our strokes. Tony jumped ashore first at the Castlecrag boat ramp, right near a sign that said, 'Beware of Sharks'.

'Did you see the *size* of that thing?' I asked. 'Did you see its *eye*?'

'No,' said Tony. 'I saw nothing. Let's go.'

Tony didn't say much as we drove home. I had to acknowledge my choice of bait hadn't been a good one. Maybe, I suggested, we could find a way to get some mullet from the fish markets and try again. But Tony didn't seem keen. After half an hour of listening to me, he said we'd be risking our lives, again. I let the matter drop. The following day he told me he had to start work on a new show and wouldn't have time to go fishing, so I changed tack and asked him to do some cover artwork for *Poetry Magazine*, which I was editing at the time. The August issue featured a silhouette based on one of his sculptures.

I left Tony alone for the next few months while he worked on his show. Then one day an invitation arrived in the mail: on one side was information about the opening of his exhibition at Gallery A, on the other a photograph of one of the featured sculptures. I was sure it was one of our fish traps—distorted and abstracted, looking just like a work of art.

Beakie — River Gar-fish

J. Sebastian Harrison
20. 4. 1998

The Magic of Garfish

My earliest memories are alive with garfish; early mornings, glassy water, light line on corks. I'd catch the tram from Neutral Bay before school and go down to Balmoral beach. The first tram was at 4 am and by the time I walked out over the wharf it was first light. All that mattered was there be no wind: even a slight breeze was a disaster. It had to do with what I call tight water, that transparent calm when you can see the fish just under the surface. When the water had that oily calmness, I always caught beakies (as garfish are called, for their elongated lower jaws). There was a special expectation like nothing else. I knew what I was doing was right, that nothing else was more important. Travelling back on the tram, surrounded by people in suits at 8 am, I'd get some strange looks. Two dozen beakies wrapped up in newspaper under one arm, and clutching a bucket containing my line and knife, smelling to high heaven.

I wonder how many fishos started off on beakies? My bet is a lot. Mention garfish and people smile. These brilliant little fish actually jump and tail-dance when you catch one on light line. They're not easy to hook, but once you get the knack you're gone. It starts at the local jetty: yellowtail (or yakkas), leatherjackets, slimy mackerel. Then you notice, beyond the swarming yakkas, out on the edges, a bobbing bit of bread crust—if it's not mullet, it's garfish. Once you have this happening, with the help of a berley of bread and tuna oil, anything can happen. I've had some of my best scraps with bonito hooked in the lip on one-kilo line this way, stripping out twenty metres of line and cutting fingers. The same thing happens with the odd kingfish or even a big slimy. It's great fishing when you're being pestered by bonito or mackerel, busted up by kingies, then when you hook up with a beakie you're happy again.

Sometimes, with the sleek, high-tech carbon-fibre rods, precision bait-casters and gelspun lines, we lose contact with the most basic things. There are times when a bit of line on a cork can outfish the most up-to-date and sophisticated gear. I mean 'outfish' here in two ways. Firstly, you catch more fish. Secondly, beakies for breakfast can't be beaten.

We took our family holiday last year by hiring a 'clipper' cruiser at Akuna Bay. Cowan Creek runs through Ku-ring-Gai Chase National Park just north of Sydney. This part of the Hawkesbury system is one of the most beautiful waterways in the country; so far it seems mirac-ulously unpolluted, and the fact that it's closed waters to professional fishing means its fish populations are pretty healthy. We anchored in sheltered bays at night with brilliant stars and woke each morning to glassy, calm green water. The inlets, bays and creeks in this system have poetic names like Castle Rock Lagoon, Yeomans Bay, Coal and Candle Creek ... All teem with a wide variety of fish: bream, tailor, flathead, whiting, mulloway, mullet, most of the baitfish and one of my favourites, beakies.

My son Orlando was with us, so I decided we'd have some fun. Instead of my usual handline and wine-cork, we used light, whippy carbon rods. With a light line and those little bubble floats that you can fill with water for some weight, these rods can put a bait anywhere. Some-times you need to—beakies usually cruise around on the outskirts of the berley cloud. They often swim with the translucent blue-coloured hardieheads; the gars have a bit more green flecked through their sil-ver-blue bodies. We found our first school at Jerusalem Bay, got up at 4 am and started berleying with bread soaked with a dash of tuna oil, and by first light our boat was surrounded by fish. Mainly yellowtail, but mixed with herring, small tailor, angelfish and the odd slimy. Out from these was a great school of hardieheads, dimpling the surface and exploding every now and again as chopper tailor made forays into the school. Then a good ten metres out from the action we could see our beakies shooting about like little blue arrows.

We were using tiny pieces of prawn for bait. Prawn is a good bait for beakies, but the flesh from a just-caught slimy is the prime bait—cut a fillet and then take little bits of flesh to fit the hook. Once you've done this the beakies are much easier to hook. We were having trouble losing baits to the myriad of yellowtail that were swarming around us, taking our baits as soon as they sank any deeper than a couple of inches under the surface. If you make the trace between the float and the hook any shorter, the bait acts unnatural; the garfish will shoot over to the bait and then shy off before taking it. I solved this problem by smearing Mucilin floatant, more commonly used in fly fishing, on the line. It worked first cast.

It was 6 am by now, but we had our first beakie tail-dancing across the tight water of Jerusalem Bay. There wasn't a lot of fish around by this stage; people in the other boats moored in the bay were waking. The odd Yamaha started warming up; some fellow walked out to the stem of his cruiser then plunged into a school of mullet. We persisted, casting our water-loaded bubble floats to where the fish appeared, always around some crust of bread, usually on the outskirts of the blue schools of hardieheads. A breeze was up by now, and Orlando was sending me up: 'Dad, it's blowing a gale.' In conditions like this beakies become difficult to hook. The thinner the number, the more timid the bite.

It's interesting to note that the mouth of a garfish is on top of its beak, unlike their big brothers, the marlin, where the mouth is under the bill or sword. I don't think this has much to do with hooking up with any of them, though it's an interesting thing to contemplate. We can certainly call garfish mini-marlin though, fished light and with the right rod: weight for weight they're definite contenders as sportfish. I haven't done it yet, but one day I'm going to make up the lightest possible fly rod and give them a go.

We eventually called it a day, and I asked Juno to photograph our catch, a grand total of three little beakies. My son was indignant when I said I was going to write a story about this pathetic effort. I said, 'No, this is what happens. I taught you it's not to do with the number or the size of the fish.' He wasn't convinced, though. All right, I thought, this means another dawn beakie expedition.

A week later I went out to Lion Island in Broken Bay. I anchored up just before dawn and berleyed. This time, no tuna oil, just bread mixed with bran; the bran floats and this mix doesn't excite the yakkas to a feeding frenzy. I just wanted to catch a few big sea-gar so Juno could take pictures for *Fishing World* and then we could eat them for breakfast. I had a point to prove, so I didn't muck about with fancy rods and reels. I caught a slimy, cut it into tiny cubes and lined them up on the edge of the board. At dawn everything was perfect, no wind, flat sea and big green beakies shooting in and out of the blue-backed slimies. No bubble float, just the handline and hook, a miniscule cube of the slimy's translucent gluey flesh. Out it sailed into the small wake at my stern created by the run-in flood tide, a billowing cloud of white bread flowing from the berley bucket.

I had my Polaroids on and the sea joined the clear sky. I watched my bait disappear as green pencil-shaped fish came from nowhere. Then the beakies were everywhere. They were jumping back out of my livebait tank, nipping around in the belly of my boat, diving into my neat coils of fishing line—which made life easy, just sitting there like cotton, no twists, no tangles, no memory.

Then a big gannet hit the water at a hundred miles an hour just out from the stem, *thwoowwopp*. It broke the spell and I looked about and realised I had a feed of fifteen silver beakies. I noticed during my trance-like hand-lining session other shapes, long pointed things with dark stripes, smaller compact turquoise torpedoes, darker shapes drifting on the outskirts of the cloud of bread. A tempting thought. This is where the bait hangs, so if I slip a pair of big red chemically sharpened suicide hooks into one of these gar and let it swim around in that white cloud of berley, well, who knows?

Chromed Monsters

It was a July afternoon last year. I'd been preparing for a night of hairtail fishing. My fishing mate had to work that day, so I was getting the boat ready to leave as soon as he got back. We knew we could make it to Waratah Bay and anchor up before dark. Juno usually comes to take photographs, but she had to attend an art gallery opening that night, so we'd have to make do with my automatic Nikon F60. Then my seaphone rang: it was John, he had to cover someone's shift. The boat was ready, I had the bait and rigs; the tide was perfect, there was absolutely no wind. Okay, I'd go alone and if I caught any hairies, I'd have to use the Nikon's timer and take self-portraits, balancing single-handed a fish that looked like a ribbon of liquid chrome, with huge predator's eyes and a mouthful of cutthroat razors.

Hairtail come to live in the river every winter. Locally they're called hairtail, but in other parts of the world they have other names: ribbon fish, cutlass fish, frost fish. My grandfather, a Hawkesbury fisherman, called them 'hairies' or 'ribbon fish' depending on his mood.

During the years of the Great Depression, families moved from Sydney and came to live in the caves at Jerusalem Bay. There are old photographs of men standing in sepia mist, holding up hairtail as tall as the humans who lived on their catches. On the shore at their feet are huge piles of fish, their silver bodies entangled. You catch glimpses of eyes, the great wide pupils of a nocturnal predator. Hairtail have teeth up to three inches long, with backwardly directed barbs, so their

Tidal Movement
at The Fork
Mooney Creek

Tidal Movement
at THE FORK   MOONEY
Creek

prey has no chance once it's been seized. The catches suited the times. Hairtail flesh was highly favoured over other available meats, such as rabbit or feral pigeons.

Taken straight from the river with their colours all lit up, their reflective skin is silver, shot through with emerald and crimson hues. They have a delicate, filmy dorsal fin running the full two-metre length of their body and ending in a slender thread. When they're feeding they swim vertically, like great ghostly seahorses suspended amid reflections.

Full-grown hairtail are around two metres long and weigh about five to six kilos. These fish can be great fun on light gear. Sometimes hooking up with a big one feels like you've caught a huge squid: they move off with a strange pulsing motion that's not quite a dead weight. But then they can really perform, sometimes slashing around on the surface. If there's no moon and there's lots of phosphorus, you see their shapes outlined as other fish follow them to the boat. They can be very cannibalistic, slashing at each other on the way up.

The bays in Cowan Creek and Coal and Candle are like great bowls of fishy soup. Some nights with mullet plopping around you, a jewie snapping its great bucket mouth shut as it rounds up its dinner just across the bay, it's hard to take when all six hairtail rods are out and their baits are soaking without a peck.

Hairtail are attracted to all forms of light. They come in from the abyss beyond the continental shelf, moving up and down the water column, searching for translucent or iridescent food, their long dorsal waving gently as they hover beneath the schools of whitebait and yakkas in the Cowan system.

This is why light sticks are so effective when incorporated into a hairtail rig. There are lots of different colours these days. I've tried them all: green, blue, yellow and red. I find the reds work much better when there is a moon and the greens on the dark of the moon.

Some writers have opined that hairtail don't swim vertically, that it's just another component of the hairie myth. It's true that they don't swim upright when they are searching for a feed or just schooling up for travelling or breeding. They do, however, swim vertically when they are taking a bait. I've actually seen them swimming upright. The water is so transparent at times in Smiths Creek at Cowan that when the light's right, just after dawn where there is absolutely no wind, and if you don't make any noise at all, you can berley them up around and under your boat. If you throw out a light line with no trace, you will be able to watch them as they take the bait.

One morning last winter I had this happening. I threw out one of my usual rigs, a set of five ganged hooks on a wire trace four inches long, and they wouldn't touch it. They were hovering and latching onto the pieces of pillies. As the little hunks of oily flesh floated down the water column, the hairies swam up and gently grabbed the flesh and moved off, but they just wouldn't take the bait on the line with a wire trace. Then I threw out a light line with no trace, with a whole pillie on it, and one of the hairies sailed over and held it and then went into this extraordinary vertical position. As soon as I saw this I understood the famous hairtail bite. In every story ever written about hairtail you'll come across variations on the theme of their strange manner of taking a bait. The first thing you notice is a light weight on the end of the line, very similar to a squid or a small crab. Then you wait. Sometimes I have had a hairie bite go on for five minutes. Just a gentle tug that doesn't even move off. This bite has been described in many ways: there has been so much written about the 'mysterious' and 'horrible' hairie bite it can be confusing until you actually experience them when they are really on the chew. It was a revelation to actually see a hairtail acting this way, and it explains all those weird 'bites' we have felt in the dead of a freezing night. They can just hang there for five minutes without moving: they hover in the water with the bait in their mouth held delicately between their fierce-looking teeth.

If you pull the bait away slowly, it activates a response and they will start to move the bait gradually into the back of their mouths. When this happens, wait until there is some tension on the line and pull a bit firmer, then they usually start to swim off. I let them take out two metres or so then hit them firmly. Sometimes hairtail will hit the baits hard, especially when you are using live bait; sometimes they swim with the bait in their mouths towards the boat and the lines go slack as if you have been bitten off. Other times they rise up to the surface and swim away horizontally. It takes a bit of experimentation; it's a matter of finding out how they are feeding on the night. Bear in mind that they very rarely hook themselves, so set rods aren't that effective. In fact, if you have trouble hooking up and get too frustrated, a handline will outfish any rod every time. The thing is, when they are timid, you have to use the right line: thin handlines and hairies mean burnt or cut fingers. A very light spinstick with a good threadline reel and a smooth drag is the most fun.

I arrived at Waratah Bay about an hour before sunset. There are about six public moorings there and if you tie up to any one of them, you're in as good a spot as any in the bay. The other bays in the Cowan system have these public moorings as well. Other top hairtail spots in the Hawkesbury system are Smiths Creek, Jerusalem Bay, Cottage Point (opposite the restaurant) and Illawong Bay.

It was a perfect night, a full moon, no wind and high tide at 8 pm. This was a night when all the factors that you usually need to catch a hairtail had come together. The tides aren't as important here as in the main part of the Hawkesbury, but the hairtail usually come on the bite around the top and bottom of the tide like most other fish. Berley is important because the hairtail are attracted to hordes of baitfish that hang around the moorings, and once you get them going, the predators start working them as well. I often catch beautiful school mulloway here among the hairtail.

It's important not to use any weight. The baits must float down as naturally as possible and, usually, the lighter your line the more fish you hook.

I caught a few yellowtail and set out a livie. I set another two rods out with pilchards on the gangs. Then just after dark I got my first hairtail bite, the light weight on the line at first, then the line started moving out. It meant they weren't playing around, they were hungry. I stood up and set the hooks. It was a hairtail; they are pretty unmistakable when you're using gelspun line. They were biting the pilchards and not touching the yellowtail. I had my first hairtail in the boat within an hour of tying up to the mooring. Often in June and July there can be up to fifteen boats with fifteen hairie crews all pulling in fish.

I wince every time I hear someone laying into one of these beautiful creatures with a huge catfish donger. Although they look fierce, once out of the water hairtail are very feeble fish: all you need to do is hold the trace in front of you and then grab them behind the head with your thumb and forefinger. This calms them down straight away. You can feel how little strength they have once they are taken out of the water.

As soon as I had the hairtail in the boat, the rod with the livebait went off. It was a jewie. In this still water, on a line without a sinker, an eight-kilo school mulloway puts on quite a show. I caught another two hairtail and then spent the next two hours taking pictures with the camera on a tripod and the timer set on thirty seconds. There were three other boats of very serious-looking hairie fishos that night in Waratah Bay. They must have had a good laugh at the weird sight of me running from the tripod back to pose at the stern of the boat, with the flashlight bouncing off a ribbon of shimmering chrome.

The Whiting

One winter afternoon I went fishing and around dusk caught a nice one. For a whiting it was quite large, fairly lean yet thick with roe; this abundance of eggs had stretched the skin, and its belly was almost transparent. The fish had swallowed my hook—traumatised, there was no point releasing it back into the wild, so I found myself killing my catch by cutting its throat. Scaled and cleaned the fish right there on the beach. As I removed its gut, I noticed without the orange roe there wasn't much flesh on the body, making it too difficult to slice into fillets. I took the whiting home and cooked it whole. There were two of us for dinner, so we picked what little flesh there was from the bones, hardly enough to satisfy, but sweet. Later on we made a fire in the grate. After a while a sleek, familiar shadow slid into the lounge room. I couldn't make out what kind of animal it was until I realised there was something of the whiting in its demeanour. As I stared the cat seemed to resemble the fish, while retaining its feline body shape. Then the animal came up to the lounge chair, rubbed itself against my leg and started to purr loudly. Although we had eaten the whiting, the presence of the fish managed to shine through this odd creature—the spirit of the whiting was alive in our new pet. A visiting friend bent over to pat the strange cat. 'Be careful,' I said, 'can't you see the poor animal is still recovering from that wound in its belly?'

Magnificent Riflebird

Towards the end of primary school, I spent a lot of time with someone I'll call Rick the Trick, an apprentice jockey who'd already, at the age of seventeen, been disbarred for fixing a race. He lived in Byrnes Avenue just down from our place. We had birds in common: Rick had racing pigeons and was a paid-up member of a pigeon-racing club at Mosman. He knew a few boys who'd been in reform school and was very proud of the fact that one of his older mates had been acquainted with the famous fence Tilly Divine.

Rick was interested in breeding birds like canaries and African love birds and selling them to pet shops. He taught me how to trap wild finches. He knew how to make intricate traps that incorporated weight-measuring scales; when a double-bar or zebra finch landed on a little platform, the scales would gradually fall until the bird was lowered into a part of the trap it couldn't escape from. Rick would place a male finch in the cage and some millet seeds on the trapdoor, then set the cage in a clearing in the bush where he knew finches lived. We'd pedal out to Epping Forest on our bikes to set these traps, generally catching a dozen or more finches on each trip, then selling them to the pet shop in Crows Nest.

We didn't just go after wild birds. 'How can anyone own a bird?' Rick would ask. 'They're part of nature. If anyone owns them, it's God, if He exists.' He'd say things like that. I was impressed. It made the kind of sense I wanted to hear. Soon we were stealing breeding canaries from aviaries around the North Shore—roller canaries and African love birds were worth quite a lot of money and the pet shops would buy them from us, no questions asked, for cash. I thought I might set myself up as a breeder when I turned fifteen and had failed at school, as I surely would. I could go into business from my own backyard. I was still drawing birds and had started keeping notebooks about them. I'd jot down notes about the birds I spotted wherever I went. I had long lists of the species I'd seen; every time I saw one that wasn't on my list, I'd enter it into my log and note the time and place.

One night I went with Rick while he raided a breeder's aviary in Mosman. I was supposed to keep watch while he stole the African love birds, but there was a shed in the backyard that warranted further investigation, and when I broke into it I discovered a pair of binoculars and a Zeiss camera: bird-watching equipment. I stuffed them into one of the sugar bags we used for carrying the birds. These bags let the bird breathe because of the loose weave, but quietened them down because they were dark inside. When we arrived back at Rick's and he opened my bag and found the camera and binoculars, he seemed angry I'd stolen them. He said they could bring us undone.

*

My marks weren't good enough to get me into North Sydney Boys High, where most of my friends went when we graduated from primary school, so I was sent to Crows Nest Technical High School instead. I found it confusing and disheartening, being surrounded by strangers and having a different teacher for every subject, and gradually slid behind, especially in maths. I bluffed my way through for as long as I could—though I knew it couldn't last forever—by copying and getting help from my friend Ray Morgan.

I somehow survived a year and a half of high school, but don't ask me how or what happened, I don't remember much—only that, because of the large class sizes, nobody noticed how little I was learning and that whenever exams were looming, I'd become so worried about my likely prospects I'd have trouble sleeping. I'd lie in bed in the early hours of the morning imagining how my mother would react when she saw my half-yearly or yearly report, and began experiencing the headaches that have plagued me ever since.

I'd daydream about burning down the school. I'd picture myself climbing in under the foundations and sitting there in the clammy dark, calculating details: how much kerosene it would take, how many loads of half-empty drums I'd have to carry there on my bike. I decided I'd strike the day I finished my exams, before they had a chance to mark them.

I must admit I found the idea of committing a criminal act appealing. But I didn't, in the end, commit arson.

From the time of my eleventh birthday, I'd grown increasingly obsessed by *Ptiloris magnificus*, which I'd read about in *What Bird Is That?* No matter how many fascinating pages I found in this book, and I found a great many, I kept coming back to the same bird, also known as the magnificent riflebird. My primary school drawings of falcons and eagles all began turning into drawings of this extraordinary creature—just as extraordinary in appearance as in name, judging by what I saw in my book.

The coloured illustration showed a plump-bodied bird that looked as though it was dressed for some sort of costume party at the palace: it had a little cap of iridescent green feathers and an elegant choco-late-coloured mask running from its long, curved beak, over its eyes and down over its shoulders. Its neck feathers were iridescent tur-quoise edged by what looked like a rope of pearls, and its breastplate might have been beaten copper, glinting in the painter's spotlight. It wore a skirt of shaggy feathers, like strands of hanging silk, and looked, compared to its relatives, huge. I wanted to find out more.

I'd never been to a public library—it wasn't something our family did – but at some point during my last year at primary school summoned the courage to cross the Bridge and went into the Mitchell. I found anything to do with officialdom or authority terrifying and was shy anyway, so I suppose you might say I slunk through the doors, then sidled over to the shelves and flicked furtively through some pages. Town planning. I looked around. There were thousands of books, every one of them possibly about town planning. I realised I'd need help.

The first librarian I approached rebuffed me, but the second—his kindlier, more maternal-looking colleague—invited me to sit at a desk and brought me a feast of first editions. I no longer remember what they were, but some of them contained illustrations by John Gould. I sat there for hours, mesmerised, taking notes, and went back several times over the next few weeks. On a hunch, I also went to the Museum of Natural History—I knew they had stuffed falcons—and, sure enough, they had a stuffed riflebird, too. It was much smaller than I'd imagined from my book, but it *was* magnificent. I sketched it, not from life perhaps, but the nearest I could get at the time.

Sometime during my first year at high school, I discovered that Taronga Park Zoo had a riflebird, down among cages I seldom went to. But its specially designed enclosure only made it seem even more frustratingly distant. I knew that if I failed my exams, as I surely would, I'd have next to no chance of ever getting my leaving certificate and becoming an ornithologist—and no chance of ever getting closer than the general public to this incredible bird. Riflebirds were rare, not like road-peckers. I couldn't just go out and get one. Unless, of course, I stole this one.

It would be like a bank robbery—possibly national news, I thought. It would certainly make the local headlines. I'd have to cover my tracks.

I'd also have to be well prepared. I'd learned at the library that riflebirds wouldn't survive in captivity without a humid atmosphere, so I'd have to provide one. I'd have to make it a nest, too—one that consisted, I'd read in my book, of a 'shallow bowl of vine-tendrils and dead leaves, lined with fine stems and twigs and ornamented around the rim with portions of snake-skins'.

I bought some snake-skins from Ray Morgan and used them to line the nest I made with stuff scavenged from Primrose and Tunks parks. As for the humidity—well, that year, Sunbeam had introduced a wonderful new frypan with a thermostat, the first of its kind, and I'd seen one through the kitchen window of one of the flats whose drainpipes I scaled in search of squeakers. I calculated that six of them under a false floor, and a drip arrangement made from a hose, should do the trick.

This particular block of flats—a fairly new one—turned out to be harbouring three of them, a bonanza! No-one seemed to be at home in any of these flats during the day. It was easy to climb up and help myself.

I made do with just those three in the end. I made tiny holes with a nail in a length of hose and rigged it so that it dripped into the frypans, which were laid out under a cage inside my pigeon coop—a cage within a cage, invisible from outside—that had a false floor I'd levelled using Dad's carpentry tools and covered with straw from the stables. It worked, though not straight away. It took more than a fortnight of trial and error. But finally I had just the steamy, sub-tropical atmosphere I wanted, the kind a riflebird might survive in.

The last touches were the mangoes and white mice. Riflebirds eat mainly insects, native fruits and berries (hence the mangoes) but sometimes, in captivity, go off these, so my bird book told me, preferring 'to kill mice and small birds and eat only the brains'.

*

The riflebird's cage was more strongly fortified than most at Taronga. It was made from glass (to retain the humidity) reinforced with wire mesh. I realised I'd need tools: a hammer to smash the glass and some wire-cutters and tin-snips to deal with the mesh. I also took a small crowbar. I put the tools in my fishing basket, tied it to my bike and strapped a fishing rod alongside. This was camouflage: if you were out late at night and the cops asked you what you were doing, fishing was okay—it was a normal, healthy pursuit for a boy, especially around Taronga, which is surrounded by some of Sydney Harbour's best and most popular fishing spots.The afternoon before, I'd stashed a cockatoo cage wrapped in hessian in some bushes near the zoo so I wouldn't have to carry it through the streets at night, which *would* have looked suspicious. If all went according to plan, I'd be leaving the zoo just on dawn and be going home in broad daylight.

I arrived at the zoo about two in the morning and went down the back towards the quarantine area, where I knew I could climb the fence. I threw the tools and cockatoo cage over first, then followed. I knew there was a night watchman who patrolled every two hours, so I waited by the cages where the riflebird was kept until he'd passed by on his round, then set to work. I didn't want to traumatise the bird or draw attention to myself by making a lot of noise, so I used the hessian to muffle the hefty whack I delivered to the glass with the hammer.

When the glass barely registered the assault—it cracked a little and buckled slightly—I panicked. I threw the hessian away and began hurling blow after blow at the glass. After half an hour or so, I did finally make enough of a hole to get at the mesh, but as soon as I felt the resistance it offered, I knew that my tin-snips were useless. Nothing short of boltcutters would be likely to have an effect. There was nothing to do but bail out.

I went back over the fence and wiped my fingerprints off the tools with my T-shirt, then hid them under some bushes. But I hadn't given up. A couple of days later, I went back to the zoo in daylight to see what they'd done about the cage. It was surrounded by a kind of barrier, like the crime scene it was—empty. I was devastated, thinking they'd moved the bird to protect it from theft. It was probably in far north Queensland by now.

But as I was leaving via my access point near the quarantine section, I heard the unmistakable *'Ya-a-s-s'* sound—'two sharp whistles' followed by 'harsh rasping notes', as described by Neville W. Cayley—coming from one of the sheds. They'd moved it to protect it, not from theft, but from louts and vandals. The quarantine area wasn't well known or readily accessible to the public and was therefore low security. My plan was back in action.

The following night I made my way back to the zoo with the cockatoo cage wrapped in its hessian cowl. I'd seen where they kept the keys to the quarantine sheds on previous expeditions, though I'd never before had a reason to use them, and collected a bunch. I couldn't believe my luck. I found the riflebird without much trouble in a hospital section in one of the sheds, where it was probably recovering from the trauma caused by my attack. It was in a special cage, designed for easy veterinary access, that slid out on a little tray and fitted snugly inside my cockatoo cage. As the sun came up, I was lugging it home. The riflebird was mine.

*

I didn't tell Ray or Rick about the riflebird. Ray wasn't all that interested in birds, and Rick would have seen it in terms of its cash value, not as a creature you'd want to study. Besides, he'd probably go off his brain if I told him I'd stolen it from the zoo. The fewer who knew the better, I decided. That meant keeping it to myself.

The house my parents rented at Neutral Bay was behind a shopfront that had been used as a factory of some kind—I seem to remember copper coils and valves—until the owner died suddenly and the factory was shut down. Nobody was using it, but the power was still connected: the electric frypans were plugged into a long extension cord that ran from my pigeon coop, down the side of the house and in through the factory door to a socket in a no-longer-locked brick storeroom. It all worked beautifully, though at first the riflebird wouldn't eat. I had to feed it with syringes I'd salvaged from the local doctor's rubbish. I gave it mixtures of fruit and crushed insects and after about a week it started eating mangoes on its own.

By now I had lots of birds: homing pigeons, racing pigeons and various kinds of finch (double-bar, zebra, firetail and Gouldian painted finches)—some of them birds I'd stolen with Rick—as well as my quails, turtle-doves, cockatiels, budgerigars and a kookaburra called Jack. I'd raised Jack from when he was a chick. He seemed to think I was his mother. I loved the idea of having the largest kingfisher in the world as a pet. Jack would sit on my shoulder and follow me round the yard as I released my pigeons and hosed Dad's vegetable garden.

One afternoon about two weeks after I'd brought the riflebird home, Jack flew into the yard next door. The lady who lived there didn't like us, and when I jumped the fence and started calling Jack, who was perched in a frangipani tree, she was outside in an instant, screaming at me to get off her garden. She looked completely baffled when he flew straight from the tree down onto my shoulder.

The next day when I came home, a grim committee was waiting for me. Our neighbour had called the RSPCA and told them I had a kookaburra with clipped wings. The RSPCA had come to investigate while I was out. My mother had invited them in and told them they were free to look around, and when they searched through the cages and found the magnificent riflebird, they rang the police, who also turned up to investigate. They called in a keeper from Taronga Park Zoo, but were less interested in the 'exotic bird' they hoped he'd identify than in the canaries and African love birds Rick and I had stolen from a bloke who turned out to be a Mosman councillor—he'd been pressuring the local detectives to find his birds.

My mother told them what she assumed to be true—that I'd caught these birds at Primrose Park—but by the time I got home, the keeper had identified the stolen *Ptiloris magnificus* and the police were fairly confident they'd found the councillor's missing love birds. They took me to North Sydney Police Station, where some detectives asked me questions. I told them I wanted to make a full confession—and did, too. I gave them all the details, as one of them typed it up, about how I'd stolen the riflebird, as well as all the others, and spilled the beans on Rick.

This was the first of a series of confessions I made to various detectives over the course of the following decade. I found it very satisfying. I remember signing the finished document with some pride, not because of the facts it related, but because—with the assistance of the police, who added their own unique jargon—I'd produced an official-looking document that would be read and taken seriously in court.

It was two weeks before my case was heard. I spent them in the Yasmar shelter for delinquent boys under the age of twelve. I remember very little about it beyond neat lawns and concrete yards and a stretch of utter darkness. There was a dormitory, too, but this is hazy.

My mother and father came with me to court, where I was charged with break, enter and steal—not just for the birds, but also for the camera and binoculars they'd found at Rick's place. He and I agreed they'd been taken by me. I was also charged with stealing a number of items I knew nothing about but nonetheless took the blame for.

Because of Rick's age, he was regarded as being the ringleader. My mother insisted it was the other way around, but when the magistrate at my hearing asked me whether I had anything to say, I parroted Rick: 'How can anyone steal a bird, Your Honour? They belong to God.'

His Honour stared at me stony-faced before frightening the life out of me by giving me a six-month sentence to Mittagong boys' home. It was through a kind of haze that I heard him tell me my sentence was suspended provided I accepted a bond to be of good behaviour for eighteen months. Yet I would end up in a boys home, and then prison, in the coming years. Sitting in a cell, far from the Hawkesbury, the birds of my childhood would flutter through the dome of my skull as mullet jumped in the black water. Of course, a bird had been my stolen goods, playing a part in my imprisonment. But birds would remain for me sources of hope and consolation, symbols of freedom.

To the Person Who Shot the White Goshawk

Who are you, in the corner of the parking lot, under the light, a white goshawk sitting on top of the pole, a squint in your eye as you take aim? Afterwards, how your sister spelled your name in the correct manner, your boss retained you, knowingly. Who walked the pedestrian crossing with that flag you waved this morning? Tell me, did your vanished wings from yesterday's life brush the tops of the hedges down the tidy street? In the trashed lane with its dismal light—was it the smell of your soul that rose from a broken pile of bricks by the waste outlet? Did you dump the T-shirt stained with bird blood in your mother's washing machine? Did your dream of flying hold you back as you did your homework? Come, let us drive out into some western place, let us bind your eyes to the sky so you can see clearly. Maybe you'll pray, though you believe in nothing at all. The eyes of a goshawk will form in a dust-cloud of nightmares for you to enter. The male's call shall not be answered and its surviving mate will rise like blurred silk into the dawn for your crosshaired desire. As the words gather in the beams of the headlights, take time, think of your act with love, learn to care for it like a hawk with its new-laid soft eggs.

A Proper Burial

The other night outside our house an owlet nightjar swooped down
onto the road after a moth. It brought to mind an encounter last
Christmas, with a pair of tawny frogmouths. Driving on the highway,
alongside the Hawkesbury River, I noticed what seemed to be an
injured bird. I pulled over and walked back to where the bird was lying
and found a tawny frogmouth had been killed on the road. I picked up
its limp body and carried it to the side of the highway, where I discovered another frogmouth, dead in a scattering of leaves. I looked
around and there was a young Aboriginal girl standing behind me. She
was wearing a white dress and seemed rather shy. I have lived here for
most of my life, but I had never met or even seen her before, so I wondered where she came from. She held out a bag and said, 'I will take
them away for a proper burial.' I asked her, 'What happened here?'
'All the cars kept going. Some ran over one of the already dead birds.
You are the only one who stopped.' She went on to explain the female
frogmouth was the first hit, then the male flew down to the side of
his mate, trying to help somehow. As the girl watched, the second
frogmouth was also run down by a car coming the other way. The girl
had walked out onto the highway and picked up one of the birds and
placed it on a bed of gum leaves by the side of the road. Then she had
gone to get a bag to carry them, which is when I turned up. We knelt
on the leaves and carefully placed both frogmouths into the used
onion bag. When it was done, the girl stood up with the bag in her
hand, then without comment walked off, heading for Mooney Point
Road. I was left standing there by the paperbarks, shaken. It had been

an upsetting experience, but somehow the girl made it easier to take. I went home with the milk I had gone out to buy in the first place. Our house was full of people, family and friends gathered for Christmas. I tried to tell my wife what happened, though it felt so out of context, a scene from another dimension. I went into my study, closed the door, and sat there going over things. Frogmouths are closer to nightjars than owls and related to both species; they're nocturnal hunters and so usually sleep by day. But these two had been run down in broad daylight. This episode, though that's hardly the right word, has never left my mind.

Bowerbird Eggs

Brett Whiteley said of all the birds he painted, the one he most resembled was the satin bowerbird. He kept a bowerbird egg in his studio and one day placed it in my hand: it was an exquisite object that felt delicate in my palm. This egg inspired several drawings, a painting and a large ceramic sculpture. I've seen a few live bowerbird eggs since, but the fragile cream, sepia-dappled egg that Brett managed to save from oblivion has imprinted itself on my imagination.

The eggs of bowerbirds are works of art. The shells have a pale Naples-yellow hue, marked with loose calligraphy; this cryptic writing is different on every egg and for every species. The eggs of satin bowerbirds have markings like drops of sepia ink fallen onto creamy paper. The great bowerbird's eggs display lines of russet pigment, a continuous writing with abstract serifs, like a painting by Mark Tobey, an open weave of intersecting lines forming an abstract tracery.

Bowerbirds are related to lyrebirds, and like them haven't changed for thousands of years; their eggs are a record of their genetic imagination. Does the female take note of the markings when she lays the eggs? Do the males admire the sepia writing on the shells when sunlight first hits the nest? Do the marks merely stain the eggs in a cryptic style so they become invisible to predators?

Satin bowerbirds have sharp sight and exceptional hearing, necessary for their world of bush and shrub with thick foliage. Their bowers are made from branches and canes woven into archways with entrances decorated with blue objects. They once gathered rare blue native fruits and feathers from parrots, but these days it's mainly blue plastic—milk container tops, pegs or drinking straws. Sometimes they include the yellow feathers from the crests of cockatoos. The male bowerbirds build these elaborate mating stages to impress and woo the females.

Bowerbirds are smart birds, and they carry out one endearing task that's especially clever: the male bird, after constructing his bower, stands back and selects a thin branch from a nearby bush and breaks it off, then stubs the end onto a rock until it splinters to form a make-shift brush. This cock-bird then dips the end of his brush into a paste of charcoal mixed with blue pigment or some ochre if it's handy, and with a final flourish, holding his paintbrush in his beak, paints the inside walls of his bower.

From the Spinoza Journal

27 November 2015

Juno was preparing to leave the river for a few days. She was flying to Brisbane for an exhibition of her photographs. I had her bags in the boot and was about to get into the car when we noticed something move on the side of the road a little past our house. It turned out to be an unfledged bird. I looked up, and there were at least five mature channel-bills in the ancient Moreton Bay fig above it. I thought the chick was a baby channel-billed cuckoo. Maybe one of these cuckoos had laid eggs in the nest and the chick was somehow kicked out. It was only a few days old, so I carefully carried it into the garage, where I placed some grass and gum leaves in the cat carrier. I gave the tiny bird several teaspoons of water and set her on the makeshift nest.

When I got back from the airport, I fed the bird a mixture of rolled oats, crushed walnut and egg yolk with a teaspoon. Our Siamese cats, Emily and Percy, gathered around the cat carrier. On seeing the chick, they didn't switch their mood to a hunting alert; instead, both cats became seemingly maternal. I fed the chick every two hours through the morning. I was relieved and happy as it gobbled up the food and drank water from the teaspoon.

Emily and Percy sat by our baby bird all afternoon and purred. I walked back outside to where I found the chick and noticed the Moreton Bay fig was laden with fruit. Figs are the main diet of

cuckoos—I picked a bunch of the extra-ripe ones, so later on I would be able to crush them into the food mix.

When you find a baby bird, the thing to do is to place it near the tree it may have fallen from and wait for the parents to turn up. I did this and watched from a distance. It was a hot afternoon, so after about an hour, I decided that was long enough. I looked around for likely foster parents—currawongs, magpies and maybe kookaburras? No action at all. I took the baby bird back inside and put it into the cat carrier. To my relief, next morning the chick was still alive and squawking for food. Percy and Emily gathered around as I fed the little cuckoo, and we all seemed to feel safe and at ease in this tentative family.

A quick note—our adopted channel-billed cuckoo chick has a name now. We decided to call him 'Spinoza' after Baruch Spinoza, the seventeenth-century philosopher. Spinoza's given name means 'Blessed' in Hebrew. Spinoza argued that God exists and is abstract and impersonal. His view of God can be described as Classical Pantheism, with infinite manifestations of divinity.

At this stage, I have worked out a diet for Spinoza the bird. Mango, boiled eggs, 'Fussy Cat' dry cat food, oats and quinoa flakes, all mixed together and blanched in boiling water to form a lumpy porridge. I feed Spin every two hours with a teaspoon. He is always hungry and squawks for more food every time I open the cage. We now have a cage because I don't quite trust the cats.

Spinoza has turned out to look like a cute little punk of a bird. Looking into his eyes, I'm sure he's lived a few previous lives. He seems to be very knowing; however, I'm not sure a channel-billed cuckoo is capable of a 'philosophy of tolerance and benevolence' like his namesake.

I watched the channel-bills in the Moreton Bay fig this afternoon. When they are in Indonesia they are known as 'fruit hawks'. They look quite sinister to me, especially when perched in a high branch against the sun; they adopt the posture of a compact vulture. There's something quite fierce in their stance. One of the birds in the great fig tree could be Spin's real parent. After laying their eggs in other birds' nests in September, they return four months later, and perform the most avant-garde version of their opera in the Moreton Bay fig; this draws their offspring away from foster parents into a family gathering. They feast on the last of the ripe figs for a few days before they all fly off together—to New Guinea! The channel-bills come down to Australia from New Guinea in summer, fly back in autumn, then eventually all the way back to Indonesia. Mature channel-billed cuckoos have wingspans that measure up to one metre and they weigh in at one kilo, which is heavy for a hollow-boned bird. They have great hooked beaks to reach the ripe fruit, similar to the hornbills.

Maybe Percy and Emily are being so friendly to Spin because they sense Spin is going to be a formidable beast. Two Siamese blue-eyed predators becalmed in the presence of this ancient philosophic bird, they sit, stare and purr. If anything, I think Spinoza is a bit of a worry to them. However, I don't trust them at all, especially Emily: they are, after all, killers.

I've been thinking of Spinoza's future. Keep a channel-billed cuckoo as a pet? Shall we return him to the wild? Spin the domestic companion would be like having Arthur Rimbaud as a pet. Verlaine discovered the result of this when he invited Rimbaud to stay at his house for a few days. Crap on the bed, the kitchen turned into a wilderness, hallucinogenic callings, songs conjuring a season in hell and, eventually, the spangled insanity echoing through a dark night of the soul.

There is a certain steely genius in the willpower of this rapidly growing, ravenous creature from the seed-highways of the world. How shall we release Spinoza to the chains of the skyway? I haven't thought too much about this yet, though already Spin's behaviour is that of a wild bird; as long as I am hand-feeding him he seems tame, but as soon as he gets a glimpse of the sky in the window he becomes agitated. This morning Spin came out from the cage and flew across the studio and jumped towards the window glass. He still can't fly and his tail feathers haven't appeared; his wing feathers have developed quickly, but I don't think he is mobile enough to injure himself. Spin would be in trouble with the local dogs if he got out at this stage. Our cats are becoming warier; they have never come across a creature like Spinoza. When they approach him, Spin makes the usual series of penetrating squawks, then an evil-sounding hiss that throws fear into the core of their feline natures.

26 December 2015

We must seriously consider releasing this young fruit-hawk back into the wild. In three months, this coming March, his real parents will turn up and perch in the Moreton Bay fig trees. By then, Spin will be fully fledged and Spin's siblings will have just about worn out the birds that hosted them. I know how they must feel—it's an exhausting and full-time job. In March, the parent cuckoos will call and call to round up their offspring for the long flight north.

These cuckoos are also known as storm birds and rain birds. My grandfather called them 'prawn birds' because their arrival signals the time of year when the Hawkesbury River prawns start running.

Their calls are raucous, some people say unearthly, especially in the night, when one is trying to sleep: an antiphonal racket that carries for kilometres. At times a dozen or more channel-bills perch in the fig tree near our house; when they call simultaneously you can hardly hear yourself speaking. They begin their avian opera with a high-pitched *kawk, kawk*, followed by *awk, awk, awk* and then a rapidly repeated *kaa-ka-ka* (which sounds like a drunken kookaburra). It's all rounded off by some general high-pitched screaming, and then a noise that sounds like a person being throttled.

Cuckoos are mysterious birds and have left behind them many myths, legends, poems, charms and ornithological records, most of them totally unreliable. Even today there are questions about where they go when they migrate and how they mate. Most of the literature is a shifting tide, like dissolving chemicals in an alchemical brew. Pliny the Elder wrote, 'The cuckoo seems to be but another form of hawk, which at a certain season of the year changes its shape.' What Pliny didn't understand was cuckoos migrated each winter; he thought they disappeared into the underground, and because they have red rings around their eyes, he gathered they had returned from Hades with eyes rimmed with 'circles of fire'.

The oldest secular lyric written in English, dating from 1250, is the 'Cuckoo Song': 'Sumer is icumen in, Lhude sing cuccu, / Groweth sed, and bloweth med, / And springth the winde nu-sing cuccu!' We understand from this song that cuckoos, storm birds, brain-fever birds, channel-bills have been driving people mad with their calls for centuries.

Charles Darwin couldn't work out where cuckoos sat in the 'scheme of things', even though they were one of his main subjects of study. He said if wrong about them, his whole theory of evolution would fall apart. However, no matter what we know about them, all the second-hand information falls away when you live with one of these near-mythical creatures. In summer at Mooney Creek, they are the loudest of birds on the Point. Inside the house every morning, I hear Spin's constant harsh call for food, a need that has to be met or there's hell to pay. Emily and Percy, who were mesmerised by Spinoza when he was a wee chick, are feeling neglected, their noses out of joint. The presence of Spin, our little channel-billed cuckoo, is very powerful.

Spinoza is growing at such a rate that each day I notice new things: his legs today, long and strong with little feather pantaloons at the top of each leg. So like a lyrebird in the way he hops about: they are related, except Spin is a perching bird and lyrebirds are ground dwelling. I notice similarities in the legs, the stance and even in gestures. It's difficult to tell how bright any kind of bird might be, that is, until you live with one: the way Spin cocks his head in attention, how his sight seems to reach all around his body, his sense of smell and taste. More than anything, though, Spin is a creature dependent on sight: colour organises his perception. Whenever he sees the colour red, his senses switch on fully. He notices the smallest fleck of red, even the tiny microdot of red light on my iPhone, he fixes onto it and then has to peck it. It's the same with coloured pegs. Spin loves the blue and the red ones most although yellow seems important, too.

I think it's to do with food: being a fruit hawk, he depends on colour to know the right fruit. According to the books I've read on cuckoos, channel-bills have a highly selective diet, eating mainly the fruit from banyan trees, along with blackberries. I haven't noticed many blackberry bushes or canes around these days, after they poisoned them in the 1960s; however, at least four ornithologists agree, the main diet is figs and blackberries. That's fairly choosey, but Spin seems quite content with chopped mango and boiled eggs today.

Last night I took a few books and a manuscript into the studio where we keep Spinoza. He free-ranges in the studio all day then I put him into a cage at dusk. He's never hungry after the sun goes down but still calls out if I am late to visit. I conduct what we have come to call 'flying lessons' for an hour or so each evening. Spin jumps onto my arm and I hold it up near a shelf and he flies between that shelf and another about four metres away. After a flying lesson for an hour, I left Spin sitting on a perch and started marking up a manuscript. After about ten minutes, Spin got tired of being ignored and flew over and landed on my shoulder. To take my attention away from the manuscript, Spin then fluttered about my face until he got the idea to bite me on the nose.

Spin suddenly seems much larger. Today he worked out how to get a wooden peg he's eyed for a few days; it was dangling on a loose end of line on which Juno hangs her photographic prints. Spinoza worked out he could pull the rope up with his claws; within a minute he had the precious peg in his beak. Every day there's a new revelation, as things I have imagined become real. I watch Spin and he bosses me around and he's only about six weeks old.

I went out after feeding Spin to see what was going on in the Moreton Bay fig tree, or banyan tree as they are called in India. I walked over to the tree, stepping softly, but as soon as I approached three or four adult channel-bills wheeled away across the bay. They look like flying crosses as they move across the sky—some books liken them to 'flying crucifixes'—and they are great flyers. They dip away from other birds gracefully but effectively in their avoidance tactics. As Pliny noticed over two thousand years ago, cuckoos 'are aware that they are hated by all the other birds; for even the very smallest of them will attack them'.

Although just about everyone who lives in Sydney has heard their midnight caterwauling, and looked to see where it emanated from, they are rarely seen, unless through a conscious effort to find them. I noticed this afternoon at twilight why this is the case: as soon as a human appears close to where they roost, they swing their whole body over the other side of a thick branch. This is why they have such powerful claws: they dig into the wood and lock onto the branch. These birds are like the outlaws in Hollywood westerns who swing over to one side of their horse, as a shield, as soon as the lawman starts shooting. This is also a power grip to hold them securely to a thick branch in a strong gale or a cyclone.

William Wordsworth wondered why he could always hear cuckoos so clearly everywhere in the Lake District but could never find them or even glimpse one: 'O blithe New-comer! I have heard, / Hear thee and rejoice: / O Cuckoo! Shall I call thee Bird, / Or but a wandering

Voice? ... To seek thee did I often rove / Through woods and on the green; / And thou wert still a hope, a love; / Still longed for, never seen'. Before Spinoza, I thought of channel-billed cuckoos in the same way as Wordsworth did, as a 'wandering Voice'.

God or Nature

for Andrew Ford

A channel-billed cuckoo in a humid tree, blinks
as lightning spears crack sky, radiance and feather
shudder and shake. A high cackled voice hits
soft paperbarks, night's blankets, raucous mating calls.

In the blue morning air tide is rising; new words
float out beneath ideas of a surface. Inside the grey
feathered head, thoughts spark shaky notes,
becoming a rehearsal for an avian libretto.

The first nation of birds with airs of flight and song
may have been inklings of human utterance,
before tight sonnet-cages containing the dark sounds
of pain expelled from a human larynx

for the desire of impossible flight, although
a drifting song passes over the cradling Nankeen Valley;
its echo, the days that refuse to pass. Days where
words form inside the head of the channel-billed cuckoo.

I'm feeling embarrassed today: I finally realised Spin is not a channel-billed cuckoo. Spinoza is a satin bowerbird! Spin is also a female, or Juno is convinced this is the case. Her plumage indicates she could be, although evidently it's difficult to tell until the bird is about five years old. If they are male, the dappled olive feathers on the immature bird's breast turn a deep indigo, feather by feather. I am relieved; the more research on channel-bills the weirder they became.

I was fixated on the channel-bills. It's all to do with words, as the poet W. S. Merwin wrote about a fat pigeon: he 'could not / Conceive that I was a creature to run from / I who have always believed too much in words'. I was calling the bird a channel bird and reading about cuckoos, without looking closely enough at the actual bird in front of me. Concerning the names for things, the philosophers, as usual, can't agree: one says you can't create a chair until you have a name for a chair, the word comes first—although you can't make a chair from language either. I was bewitched by the profusion of channel-bills that arrived at Mooney Creek last spring. I projected this presence and my obsession with cuckoos and their names onto Spinoza the bowerbird.

Channel-bills are dark creatures, and no matter how hard I tried to appreciate their survival tactics, they were beginning to seem quite sinister as I watched the adults in the Moreton Bay fig tree. I am relieved I don't have to live with a bird that weighs a kilo and has a wingspan reaching a metre in length. I thought Spin was a baby cuckoo thrown out of her nest, but I read later that this rarely happens. More likely Spin, the baby bowerbird, was squeezed out from her nest by a large stepsister or brother channel-bill and the step-parents were too exhausted to feed any more chicks.

Spin was so tiny and featherless she was hard to identify, and I made a wild guess without thinking. My head was full of brain-fever birds, fruit hawks and storm birds; I became fixated on Spin being a cuckoo. I'm a bit rocked because I'm usually okay identifying birds. The good news is that Spin's a seven-week-old female bowerbird and

I'm overjoyed. Spin's own flock visits our backyard often and now I don't have a bird that will need to take the long migration. Spin is a river girl.

12 March 2016

What a rough time we've all been through this last month or so. I've been unwell for months, and Juno rang the ambulance just in time. I spent two weeks in hospital with pain in my chest and lesions on my legs from vasculitis (cryoglobulinemia), a secondary condition created by hep C virus. While I was in hospital, Juno took loving care of both me and Spin. During the first week of my hospitalisation, Juno and Spin bonded and now Spinoza has two very close human parents. I am on the mend after a course of a new wonder drug, 'Harvoni'. My viral load is now undetectable, and the vasculitis is under control with the treatment of huge doses of prednisone. When I came to in hospital all I could think of was how Juno and Spinoza were going. It was a scary time and thanks to great doctors I pulled through. One doctor told Juno, after my release, that he wasn't sure I'd come out of the hospital. So it was all fairly terrible. When I was ill I would wake up in the mornings feeling like I'd just climbed out of the abyss; but I'd look at my watch and after downing my tablets I'd be up because I had to tend to Spinoza. Spin was always so pleased to see me, jumping out of the cage and onto my shoulder and gently pecking my nose or lips.

Spin flies across the studio and into Juno's darkroom and has created her first experimental 'bower', arranging pegs used for drying photographic prints. It may be a while before she can fly into the garden because her tail feathers haven't grown long enough yet and she finds it difficult to navigate her landings. I have to do more research on how to go about creating what bird people call a 'soft release' for Spin. I intend to consult with a bird doctor who has been recommended and the ornithologist at Taronga Zoo. Meanwhile, Spin is thriving on the diet I have created for her and the daily 'flight school' takes care of her exercise. Whenever I try to read a book in the studio, Spin throws pegs at me to get my attention, like a child who needs to be watched each time she does something new. Every day her eyes seem to absorb more shades and kinds of blue; the blue colour of her irises is quite startling.

*

House-glow, the night outside,
here the kitchen light reflects
electric splinters, uncountable
shards clustered in a blue eye.
—'Looking into a Bowerbird's Eye'

19 September 2016

Juno is in Umbria, Italy, participating in a photographic workshop at Monte Castello di Vibio. She has been gone for three days now and Spin looks for her each morning. Today Spin decided that Juno had be somewhere in the studio. She flew into the darkroom then hopped about, checking every alcove and crevice, paying attention to the bottles of chemicals and the print washing trays. She landed on the Leica enlarger and decided to tweak one of the calibrating knobs with her beak. She searched under the benches and started rustling through Juno's papers and negative files. Later, I went back into the studio to check. There she was, perched in her cage, looking at the native willow outside the bay window, one eye on a king parrot, the other checking for boats on the river.

Spin's eyes followed the movement of the parrot, and I recalled a couplet from William Blake: 'A Robin Red breast in a Cage / Puts all of Heaven in a Rage'. Our time together is precious. We can't keep her as a pet too much longer. Spin needs to fly with a flock of her own kind and socialise with birds, not people, to build bowers or nests. The male bowerbird builds bowers. The female bowerbird builds nests.

Wild birds brought up by humans can't be released into the wild. Spin would have imprinted Juno and me as her parents by now. If released she would look for us, or other humans; she'd be vulnerable to predators because she has not learned to avoid them. Spinoza has no sense of fear. The noisy miner birds would mob her and currawongs would attack her. The only solution we have left, after missing the chance for a 'soft release', is to offer Spin to the ornithologists at Taronga Zoo. They have an expansive rainforest aviary there; you can walk through it and watch other handraised bowerbirds in the trees and thick shrubs and ferns.

*

Returning home from Brooklyn today, on the marshy land near the playground, I passed a family of plovers: walking, bobbing, then flying almost vertically up into the sky with their high squawking alarms. At other times, standing on one leg, flashing their spur-wings, wearing oriental masks, moving as you approach, preferring to power walk rather than to fly, until absolutely necessary—always near some form of water, preferably a puddle, a small pond, a dripping tap. Always sticking to their land claim, a small area of plover lore and sacred ground. Plovers make me feel calm, almost peaceful. They cause me to smile as I pass by their antics as they protect their chicks, broken winged dancing, dragging themselves across the grass, distracting, always distracting, and ready to fend off their young's enemies, no matter how large or fierce. With sepia wings, chrome-yellow masks, wattles and white breasts, they are noble birds, omens of hope. Although they mainly walk off when approached, they can also attack and swoop you if they have eggs or young chicks. Plovers are excellent flyers whenever they feel like it.

1 April 2017

After a good night's sleep Spinoza returned to her daily routines today and seemed very happy. Last night, not long after Spin's escapade in the wild, I went into Juno's studio. Spin had fallen to sleep on one leg on the bookcase. Usually, I just hold out my hand and she jumps on, then I take her into her night cage. Last night when I held out my hand, she woke but shook her head: I could tell she was in some vast dream about bottlebrush trees and noisy miner birds. Then she jumped into her cage and perched and fell asleep, exhausted but satisfied. Today, when I took her out into the garden for some sun, Juno said. 'You're out of your mind! Spin will just open the catch on the holiday cage and get out again.' Just as well Juno mentioned this. I tied the catch together with some strong white cord. Spin was delighted to be back in the garden and she didn't seem interested in getting out at all. She hopped around in her cage, and whenever the noisy miner birds came by, she squawked at them, happily protected by her cage. And when 'the enemy' (a local feral river cat) turned up, Spinoza was defended by Percy and Emily; they came pelting down the veranda, their fur standing on end, yowling like demonic Siamese banshees, until the enemy turned and took off at top speed and vanished into the bush. Saved by her familiars!

I went into the studio to give Spinoza some breakfast this morning and greeted her with 'O Spin!' She usually doesn't answer in the mornings, but today she repeated the last word she said to me yesterday afternoon, enunciating each syllable beautifully: 'Today'. The ornithologists in my first bird books, including *What Bird Is That?*, regarded bowerbirds as being closely related to birds-of-paradise. Based on contemporary molecular evidence, these days they say, yes, bowerbirds are part of the corvid family of Australia–New Guinea; however, bowerbird DNA indicates they are more ancient and are closer relatives to lyrebirds. So it's not surprising that Spin is so vocal and can speak human words so easily, not to mention her meowing and Siamese keening in cat language when she speaks to Percy and Emily.

Spinoza spent most of the day in the dappled sunlight of the garden. She jumps into her portable 'holiday cage' on the days she wants to go out from the studio, and I take her to a shady spot under the bottlebrush tree. Spin is proving to be as popular with the other birds as she is with humans. Her gentleman caller came and she squawked him away; but then a gentle crested dove I have named Max Ernst came down to visit and consoled Spin. Spinoza is very keen on Max and a great friendship is developing. He performed a fan dance around Spin's corner of the garden, jumping from the ground onto the wires and singing *whoo, who, woop*. Spin answered with 'O Spin', 'Whisper' and 'Spina', as well as some deep-sounding bowerbird language beyond human comprehension. Max grew very excited and kept repeating, 'Who, who'. Spin finished off with six pips at about one-second intervals, a perfect recital of Radio National's Time Signal.

Two of Bluebeard the Bowerbird's wives appeared, in the branches above the cage; one landed on the wire, and the two of them were getting on for a while until some disagreement came up and the sister-wife flew off. Spin was very happy with her visitors and performed an array of imitation songs—noisy miners, a currawong, even

some magpie fluting and the harsh cat-like call of her own composition, along with human whistling and a few words. It was a sunny
afternoon of company and paw-paw refreshments.

7 June 2017

It was too bleak and cold this morning for Spinoza to enjoy the garden, so we stayed inside. It was even too chilly in the studio. I decided to turn the heater on while I did some work on my laptop. I didn't want Spin to get a cold, so I had the heat turned down to its lowest level. After checking it out, Spin decided she wanted more of this lovely warmth, so jumped on top of the heater and turned the heat gauge up with her talons (she had studied me turning it on earlier). Then she bent over to see if the hot air was coming out stronger and, pleased with her effort, she jumped down in front of the heater and enjoyed the stream of hot air, puffing up her feathers.

Then, in the afternoon, Spinoza had great fun teasing Percy and Emily. They kept looking in through her window, gazing at her with their blue eyes. So Spin turned it on and gave them a show: with a piece of torn paper in her beak, she whistled and spoke to the cats for a good ten minutes, 'O Spin' and 'Spina'. She kept repeating 'Today' and 'Yes'. It was so funny and revealed Spin's wicked side. The cats were quite puzzled, looking through mosquito screen, their noses pressed up against the windowpane, bewildered again.

21 July 2017

Bluebeard the Indigo Beast—Bluey the male bowerbird turned up again. Today he came swooping into the garden and landed on the roof of Spinoza's garden cage. He chased off the king parrots, sang to Spinoza, then stole one of her grapes! He proceeded by trying to woo Spin at twilight. Spin was more interested than usual, but then Bluey flew off as one of the cats came slinking along the pathway. After I put Percy indoors a sweet female king parrot came down to console Spin for a few minutes, then the dreadful screeching wives of Bluey came tumbling out of the guava tree and continued to abuse poor Spin for having the hide to flirt with their Bluey. These nasty sister-wives would have torn Spin apart if she hadn't been protected by her cage. It was getting dark, so I took Spin back into her studio and we had a cup of tea together as she spoke to me about her afternoon. She mainly said, 'Today' and 'Whisper' and 'No peck', and finally she repeated 'O Spin' and 'Spina' several times. Spin listened to some of Richard Glover's radio show *Thank God It's Friday* and afterwards fell asleep on her library perch standing on one leg.

It's the beginning of bower-building season for bowerbirds.

10 August 2017

There seem to be two Bluebeards! First old Bluey turned up with two blue milk caps for Spin: he performed his ritual and flashed the bluetops about until it drove Spin so crazy that she responded with her one-winged dance. Then, suddenly, another Bluey appeared in the olive tree and soared down to the yard, where he pranced about like a pretender until the first Bluey took off and flew away. The mature male bowerbirds are tricksters as well as outrageous flirts and lovers. By the time a male's plumage turns indigo, it has built many a fancy bower and wooed many a young, olive-backed beauty like Spin.

Peter Rowland writes in *Bowerbirds*: 'In captive situations, bower-birds have even killed other bird species such as Superb Fairy-wrens (*Malurus cyaneus*), to use their blue feathers as decorations. Blue feathers are among the most highly prized decorations.'

Spinoza had a multitude of visitors today: a currawong, some crested doves, rainbow lorikeets, along with a couple of kookaburras, who laughed all afternoon at the spectacle of birds and cats. Max turned up, along with an army of surrealists. Even Percy and Emily went down into the yard to try the food on offer. They became confused by the vegetarian spread, so circled the blue dish in bewilderment as the birds flew off. Spin kept talking to the cats: 'No peck', 'Today', 'O Spin' and other excited mutterings.

30 August 2017

Springtime on Mooney Creek. The first blue-tongued lizard of the year turned up this morning. Enjoying the new wood chips Juno had delivered yesterday, the lizard basked on the surface, gathering heat from the sun in the garden. With much excitement as Spin sounded the alarm, Percy and Emily couldn't resist checking out the blue-tongued lizard, who slowly slid to safety under the house where the cats can't manage to venture. On the veranda, a light wind ruffled my notes.

23 September 2017

The first day of real summer weather and Spinoza spent the morning in the garden. After midday, when it became too hot and windy, I brought her up onto the veranda where she loved watching Juno going through her papers. Griffo arrived by boat and came up from the jetty with his dog Jumbo in his arms. Spin was very pleased to meet a new animal, and soon they were getting on just fine, except Emily became a bit jealous at one stage and meowed for attention. Then Juno and I retired with Spin into her studio, where we took photos on my iPhone as we passed it back and forth. Finally, I passed Percy and Emily on the veranda, stretched out and looking exhausted by all the action during the afternoon. They need to recover now so they can watch the twilight arrival of the king parrots and cockatoos.

29 September 2017

Spin's Picnic! I cleaned out Spinoza's studio today and had the idea to throw a picnic for Spin's friends. I put apple, chopped celery and carrot, along with bird seed, in the garden in front of Spin's cage. The cockatoo came down from the bottlebrush tree and sat on Spin's cage to observe the festivities. Spin was very happy; Juno and I sang her Jimmy Webb's song 'Wichita Lineman', her favourite song. There were four grapes in the food dish, and of course Bluebeard ate the lot.

Late morning, a beautiful shining crow came to visit Spin: it had a magnificent mane and went strutting around the backyard, too big for Emily to pretend to stalk, while Percy decided to stay on the veranda and stick with a low profile. Afterwards, with Spin back the studio, I cleaned her cage and changed the water. Boiled egg and parsley for lunch, Spin's favourite form of protein aside from cabbage moths that stray into her reach.

2 April 2018

Spin's Easter report. Spin is in great form this week. His leg seems completely healed. The final stage is regrowth of the scale on the outside of the leg and this is going well. Spin is almost always using both legs now. This helps with preening and general grooming and has resulted in a much friskier mood.

Spinoza is three years old and has begun the change that comes to all immature male bowerbirds. All immature bowerbirds look like females, which accounts for our confusion. However, when a male reaches maturity, his plumage turns indigo, with the sheen from which a satin bowerbird gets its name. Usually this occurs when they are five years old: evidently, Spin is an unusual bowerbird in every way. He is molting, and the light olive and sepia feathers are being replaced with dark indigo plumes. They have become very fine on his body, almost like fur, and Spin's wing and tail feathers are very strong. Also, Spin's beak has changed colour from black to cream, and this ivory will gradually gather a bluish tint.

I notice Spin's tail feathers are sometimes split at the tips—like a bird's version of split ends. The feathers are remarkably resilient. When Spin is not in top form—when he is unwell—his tail and wingtips fray and split apart. Then after he has a bath and sits in the shady sunshine for a couple of days, the feathers interlock again and shine with tone. Brown or dark feathers are stronger than pale plumage.

Spin was in a lovely mood today in my study. I was working on the manuscript for my new book. As I look into Spin's eye, when he turns his head to one side, I sense an empathy between us. When Spin gets tired of hovering, flitting and flying across my study, pecking books around the desk and picking up blue pencils, he flies into his carry cage and lets me know he wants to go back to Juno's studio. Then Spin can settle on his nocturnal perch before dark and catch a good twelve hours sleep each night.

For lunch Spin had two black prince cicadas, a cup of green peas, and mixed fresh herbs and celery. A drink of water and some mixed bird seed and blueberries for dinner. Then a big splashy bath to cool down before turning in for the night.

15 *October 2018*

Spin has managed to sprain his leg and the old wound has been playing up. His leg was bleeding last week, for only a few minutes, but it really worried me. It was quite a fright for both Spin and myself. When he noticed the blood from his leg dropping onto the floor, he stopped and stared at the little pool, then studied it carefully for a minute or so. I was relieved when the bleeding stopped.

After two days of peaceful time in the studio, the leg is improving. Yet the injury shows that Spin wouldn't last long in the wild. It's been over two and a half years since the first wound from the fall from the nest near the channel-billed cuckoos, and one and a half years since the noisy miner birds attacked Spin in the bottlebrush tree—and the wound flares up every time Spin lands in an awkward manner. I always feel sad at times like this, because when Spin is in top form, I imagine him joining the flock that still visits in the garden.

Although I have loved birds all my life and love Spin deeply, it is Spin who has taught me that birds are nothing at all like humans. They are far removed from us, really, except that sometimes they let us project ourselves onto what we imagine them to be.

*

In the old days I used to think art
That was purely imagined could fly higher
Than anything real. Now I feel a small fluttering
Bird in my own pulse, a connection to the sky.
—from 'The Kingfisher's Soul'

Ptilonorhynchus violaceus
(feathered beak)

First Sighting

When we set out the nets, my father would say, 'Every second counts.' In those days we fished for blackfish, flathead and bream, but mainly caught mullet. After setting the nets we'd camp on the shore and wait for the cork-line to vibrate, until it started to shudder as the fish began to hit the mesh. This night we were fishing the upper reaches of Middle Harbour in a bay off Primrose Park. I was a kid, with a chaff bag wrapped around my shoulders, looking out from under a lantana bush. Some creature made a hissing noise, then gurgled like the devil drinking hot rum from the lid of a thermos. The dawn was breaking, so I waited quietly, looking towards the noise. Bushes rattled and split apart. A plump indigo bird jumped down from a branch, hopped over to a clearing, then nodded and twitched its head in a series of rapid jerky movements. I decided to stay still as possible and wait to see what would happen. When the shiny bird noticed that I was there too, it was on the ground, just inches away from my head. I saw the jewelled eyes of a male satin bowerbird. The first one I'd seen beyond the pages of a book. I was gripped by its strange, charged reality. The image of a bird with cobalt eyes imprinted itself on my memory, and it has stayed there for keeps.

Afterword

In July of 2022, following a pattern of several decades, my family and I visited Robert Adamson and his wife, the renowned photographer Juno Gemes, at their home on Cheero Point, on the Hawkesbury River north of Sydney. One memorable morning we all set out in their boat, *The Swamp Harrier*, past the Brooklyn wharf and Little Wobby, past the broad opening to the Pacific Ocean, and through Cowan Creek to America Bay. We dropped anchor beneath a tree where a pair of whistling kites were whistling sweetly and we fished a little, catching two small bream to take home for the cats. A waterfall from recent winter rains poured down the sandstone escarpment. We ate bread and cheese, talking through the morning. Bob spoke of rowing to this bay in his youth, and on to Jerusalem Bay, a favourite fishing spot and the subject of his first fully finished poem: 'Whipbirds in needle-frost surge on the tidal mist, ventriloquists / down the corridors of morning'. Only much later would we realise that it would be Bob's last fishing trip, his last time on the Hawkesbury, which had occupied so much of his life and imagination. In retrospect, it was a season of last things with him: a few days later, he would give his last poetry reading, at Brett Whiteley Studio in Surry Hills.

Throughout that July visit, we talked of a final book and what shape it might take. Since finding Spinoza as a bowerbird chick in 2015, Bob had been making notes towards a work of prose tentatively titled *Spinoza, the Bird Who Fell to Earth*. Despite masses of research and journal entries, the intended book had stalled, caught between the daily routines of raising a wild bird and the narrative arc he sought. While Bob was recovering from treatment for hepatitis C, Spinoza had structured his days and brought his energies into focus. But under the demands of a growing bird, and his own fragile health, his writing had consisted mainly of luminous fragments: recipes for mash, quotes from ornithologists, pencil sketches, and records of the words Spin had learned through eerie mimicry. With only a few dozen pages of revised journal entries, Bob had begun to broaden the book's scope to include other writing he had done on the natural world through the years—essays written for *Fishing World*, along with prose poems and excerpts from his autobiography. The book would collect his finest prose on animal life.

Fishes swimming through the Hawkesbury, and birds flying above it, set the rhythms of Bob's life. They were extensions of his self, at once alien and familiar. Through his real and imaginative engagement with these creatures, he often explored the tension between freedom and captivity. In childhood, his love of birds led him to catch them, and his theft of a bird led to his own incarceration. Yet they remained for him 'symbols of freedom'. In a similar fashion, Bob would sometimes describe a deep ambivalence about fishing, in which getting close to the mauve-silver body of a mulloway involves killing it. As he writes in one of his greatest poems, 'The Gathering Light':

Time whistles around us, an invisible
flood tide that I let go
while I take in what I have done.
It wasn't a fight, I was drawn to this moment.
The physical world drains away
into a golden calm.

The sun is a hole in the sky, a porthole—
you can see turbulence out there,
the old wheeling colours and their dark forces—
but here on the surface of the river
where I cradle the great fish in my arms
and smell its pungent death, a peace
I've never known before—a luminous absence
of time, pain, sex, thought, of everything
but the light.

If such poems achieve a visionary intensity, outside of time, Bob's prose finds an easy precision borne of long familiarity with his subjects. His keen observations are also companionable, conveyed with sympathy and humour. As in John Clare's writing, delicate perceptions get expressed in sensual diction and description: the 'oily calmness' of 'tight water', the 'gibbering' teeth of a mulloway. When the writer casts his line into the landscape, his language is attuned to the rod's slightest vibrations, quietly attentive and alert.

Through August and September, we worked on *Birds and Fish* (as it had come to be called) through email, editing and arranging the pieces. Once Bob had been diagnosed with liver cancer, the project took on new urgency: doctors gave him only weeks to live. In December, I paid a last visit, with a rough manuscript for this book in my bag. When I arrived, Bob's health was in a steep decline and he could barely walk. On December 13, Juno, John Griffiths and I moved Bob into hospice at Neringah. He had the chills when we reached the facility, and joked, 'I feel like I'm in Jerusalem Bay at half past six in the morning.' Even after leaving the Hawkesbury, it still ran through his veins and metaphors. The next day, we read through his manuscript, giving shape to the Spinoza material, selecting the journal entries to include. After hours of talk—of sentences and paragraphs, cuckoos and bowerbirds, mulloway and garfish, the 'shining incidents' of his life—we left Bob lying in his bed, happy yet exhausted. He slipped into a long sleep, then passed away at 1 am on Friday, 16 December 2022.

Devin Johnston

Acknowledgements

Portions of this book have been revised from previous publications: 'Birds and Fish', 'Nets and Traps' and 'Magnificent Riflebird' from *Inside Out: An Autobiography* (Text, 2004); 'Mulloway on the Dark of the Moon', 'The Magic of Garfish' and 'Chromed Monsters' from *Fishing World*; 'After the Deluge', 'The Whiting' and 'A Proper Burial' from *Net Needle* (Black Inc., 2015); 'First Sighting' from *Meanjin*. 'Looking into a Bowerbird's Eye' and 'The Kingfisher's Soul' are quoted from *Reaching Light: Selected Poems* (Flood Editions, 2020).

Thank you to Paul Sheehan for helping to organise notes on Spinoza, and to Matthew Holder and Emma O'Donnell for editorial assistance in preparing this manuscript. Undoubtedly, the author would wish to thank John Griffiths for his friendship, for never forgetting the bait, and for caring for Spinoza during difficult times. Most of all, he would thank Juno Gemes for her love and care.

About Upswell

Upswell Publishing was established in 2021 by Terri-ann White as a not-for-profit press. A perceived gap in the market for distinctive literary works in fiction, poetry and narrative non-fiction was the motivation. In her years as a bookseller, writer and then publisher, Terri-ann has maintained a watch on literary books and the way they insinuate themselves into a cultural space and are then located within our literary and cultural inheritance. She is interested in making books to last: books with the potential to still be noticed, and noted, after decades and thus be ripe to influence new literary histories.

About this typeface

Book designer Becky Chilcott chose
Foundry Origin not only as a strong,
carefully considered, and dependable
typeface, but also to honour her late
friend and mentor, type designer Freda
Sack, who oversaw the project. Designed
by Freda's long-standing colleague,
Stuart de Rozario, much like Upswell
Publishing, Foundry Origin was created
out of the desire to say something new.